The Girl That No One Claimed

By: Paige Johnson

The Girl That No One Claimed

Copyright © 2025 by Paige Johnson

This is a work of nonfiction based on the author's personal experiences.
Some names, identifying details, and certain events have been changed or combined to protect the privacy and safety of individuals.

First Kindle edition: 2025

Content Warning

This memoir contains descriptions of child abuse, sexual abuse, domestic violence, trauma, and emotional neglect. Some scenes may be distressing or triggering for readers. Please take care while reading and step away if you need to.

Dedication

For every child who learned to stay quiet to survive.
You were never meant to carry it alone.

Author's Note

The events in this book are drawn from my own
life and memories. While I have done my best to
tell the truth as I experienced it, memory is
imperfect, and some details have been changed,
condensed, or left out to protect privacy and safety.

Because of legal proceedings and for my own
protection, my name was changed by the state when
I was a minor. In these pages, I write under the
name I choose for myself now.

If you recognize parts of this story, it is not an
invitation to confrontation. It is simply my right to
speak about what I lived through, in my own words.

Contents

PROLOGUE

Before I Existed

***

Before I ever took a breath, there were already secrets moving through my bloodline.

On my mother's side there was steel and silence.

Her father was a union man, the kind whose name meant something in the halls where deals were made. People spoke about him in half-whispers and half-pride. When he drank, stories slipped out in crooked pieces about strikes and threats, about men you didn't cross twice.

My grandmother was the opposite of quiet. She was sharp and strange and too smart in a way that made people nervous. Back then they didn't have many words for a woman like her. They called it "nerves" and "episodes" and said she had "mental problems," like that explained anything. Now I think she was simply wired differently—bright and overloaded, born in the wrong time. When I was little, Thanksgiving was at her house.

In the living room, there was a tiny glass bottle with a miniature doll trapped inside. I'd stand by the window, turning it in the light, trying to find the angle that might let her escape. Outside, a koi pond waited dark and deep in my memory, orange fish gliding under the water like moving coins. I was certain if I fell in, I'd sink forever and never hit bottom.

My cousin Todd and I ran through the woods behind the house, shoes catching on roots, breath burning in our chests. Out there, no one was shouting. No one was forgetting us. We could pretend we belonged somewhere else entirely.

Later I found out those Thanksgivings were already the end of something.

My grandmother got brain cancer. It came fast and cruel. She ended up in a wheelchair, her eyes dimmer but still seeing more than she ever said. The last Thanksgiving there felt heavy in a way I didn't have words for. Everyone moved slower. Laughed softer. Like the whole house knew it was saying goodbye.

She died in 1981. After that, the holidays moved to my Aunt Janet's, and the pond, the woods, and the bottled doll turned into ghosts that only I seemed to remember.

On my father's side there was war.

My dad, Roy, had been a tunnel rat in Vietnam—small and fast and just crazy enough to crawl into the dark under the earth where enemies hid.

He didn't talk about it often. But when he did, his voice went flat and far away, like he was standing in two places at once: half in our kitchen, half back in some suffocating tunnel.

He told me once about dropping into the ground with two friends and climbing out without them. About a woman in a tunnel with a gun and two children pressed behind her, pulling the trigger because that was the only choice she'd been given.

In his version, nobody was innocent and nobody was entirely guilty. There were just people stuck in something bigger and meaner than they could understand.

One day, after one of those missions, his sergeant ordered him back down. My dad refused. The sergeant hit him. My dad hit back.

That's when he said he "left his emotions at home." There was no home there to leave anything at, of course. What he meant was that feeling too much got you killed. If not your body, then whatever part of you still believed the world was mostly good.

When the war spat him out, the country didn't know what to do with him. He carried training and reflexes that didn't fit anywhere quiet. So he found the places that weren't quiet.

The underground.

My mother had her own ghosts long before I ever existed.

She got pregnant at sixteen. Her parents sent her to a Catholic home for unwed mothers, a place built more for erasing girls than helping them. She gave birth there. A doctor adopted the baby. No baby shower. No nursery. Just silence and paperwork and a hole she carried around afterward.

My mother never talked about that child to me. She carried the absence like a stone in her pocket.

By the time she met my dad, she was pregnant again—this time by a biker who rode in, left a heartbeat growing inside her, and kept going. That baby became my older half-sister, the one who'd be there on our road trips, the one my dad raised even though she wasn't his by blood.

My mother moved through all of this with a tight jaw and sharper edges. She was beautiful in the kind of way that made people lean in without ever wondering what it had cost her to stay standing. She learned early that feelings were liabilities. She passed that lesson down the only way she knew how: by refusing softness.

My parents met in the overlap between their worlds my mother's father's union halls and my father's after-the-war hustles.

By then, Dad had built a life out of what he was good at: risk, engines, and survival. He grew weed taller than I would eventually be. He built custom motorcycles that roared like anger given chrome. He raced anything with an engine and did favors for people who didn't write things down.

He barely drank; He didn't use. His addiction was speed and danger.

My mother worked in the automotive plants—steady and sharp, her life tied up in production lines. Her father's influence and my dad's hustle crossed paths, and somewhere in that tangle they decided they were a match.

Two broken people with old wounds and no blueprint for gentleness.

No one showed either of them how to love. They only knew how to hold on, fight, and endure.

So that's what they did with each other and with me.

I was born in the middle of all that, in the heat of a Michigan summer, the air thick and storm heavy. Somewhere outside, someone was mowing a lawn and swatting mosquitoes, living a perfectly ordinary life.

Inside a state hospital outside Detroit, my mother was not okay.

They said she couldn't hold me the way mothers do in movies. She didn't look at me like a miracle. She looked at me like a reminder: of the baby she'd lost at sixteen, the life she never wanted, and the man I was tied to that she'd grow to hate.

My dad took me from that hospital and placed me in the arms of his older daughter, Shirley. For the first six months of my life I lived with Shirley and my grandmother like a doll passed into steadier hands.

My mother stayed behind to "get better."

When she finally came home, I was handed back like property returned after a repair.

From the outside, I'm sure it looked like a fresh start:

Mother. Father. Children. Horses. House.

But by the time I was old enough to walk, I'd already inherited a bloodline of silence, anger, and survival.

I didn't know that within a few years my mother would ride a horse straight at me across the yard.

And that would be the first time I understood how dangerous it was to be the girl nobody really wanted to claim.

PART I

LITTLE GIRL IN THE CHAOS

CHAPTER ONE

The Day the Horse Ran Me Down

***

My first clear memory is dirt.

I'm six years old, sitting in the middle of the flowerbed my mother tried to care about before she stopped trying about most things. Railroad ties frame it in a rough square. The flowers are mostly dead now, but to me it's still magic my own private island of dust.

The summer air is heavy enough to sit on. Cicadas whine in the trees. Somewhere on the property a horse snorts and stamps, but that's just background noise. Horses have always been there, like the smell of cigarette smoke and motor oil and the constant hum of something about to go wrong.

I drag a stick through the dry soil, drawing crooked roads that go nowhere. My bare legs are streaked with dust. My hair sticks to the sweat on the back of my neck.

For a few minutes, nobody is yelling. Nobody is calling my name. Nobody needs anything from me. I'm just a little girl in the dirt, making pretend roads out of a place where nothing really grows.

Something taps at the edge of my attention: a distant rhythm, dull and steady.

Hooves.

I don't look up.

We always have horses moving in and out of the yard. They're loud and bigger than anything that should trust people. But they trust my mother. Or maybe they're scared of her too.

"Lena! Get out of my flowerbed!"

Her voice slices through the air, sharp and irritated.

I don't move. I don't even register the words. Six-year-old ears are selective, and right now the stick in my hand is more important than whatever she's complaining about from across the yard.

My sister's scream gets to me first.

"Lena, move!"

I lift my head.

My mother is already coming.

She's astride Handy, her Tennessee Walker, body pitched forward, hair blown back. The horse is at a full run, eating the distance between us with long, furious strides. Dirt flies up from under his hooves.

For a split second I'm frozen, my brain lagging behind my eyes.

She'll stop, I think. She has to stop.

She doesn't.

Her face is set, jaw tight, eyes narrowed—not wide with fear like a mother whose child is in danger, but thin with anger, like I'm the danger.

"Mom?" I whisper, too quietly for anyone to hear.

There's no time to scramble out. No time to decide which direction is safe. Handy hits the edge of the flowerbed, hooves slamming into the railroad ties. Wood jars. The world lurches.

Something hard slams into my shoulder.
The sky flips.

I fly sideways, small body caught in a storm of wood and dirt and horse.

The breath blasts out of my lungs when I hit the ground. For a second I can't remember how to breathe at all. The world contracts to a high-pitched ringing and a blur of light.

I taste dirt and copper.
My chest spasms, hunting for air that won't come.

From somewhere far away I hear my sister screaming again.

"Oh my God! Dad! DAD! She ran her over!"

Hands and hooves and sunlight spin in my vision. I roll to my side, choking, the first ragged gasp finally clawing its way into my lungs. The air burns all the way down.

Through the haze, I see my mother.

She hasn't thrown herself off the horse. She hasn't dropped to her knees to check if my bones still line up right under my skin. She sits there, turning Handy lazily, looking down at me with mild annoyance, like she's stepped in something she didn't want on her boots.

Our eyes meet.

"Maybe she'll listen next time," she says, her voice flat.

Then she digs her heels into Handy's sides and rides away, leaving me crumpled in the wreckage of her flowerbed.

Kara reaches me first, sneakers skidding in the dirt as she drops to her knees.

"Lena! Oh my God, are you okay?" Her hands hover over me, afraid to touch, afraid not to.

I wheeze, sucking in another jagged breath. My chest feels like someone parked a truck on it.

Boots pound across the yard.

My dad.

He takes in the scene in one fast sweep—broken flowerbed, dust hanging in the air, my sister crying, me half-curled on my side.

And my mother, trotting away on her horse.

Something in his face breaks.

He doesn't ask what happened. He doesn't sort through blame. He runs after her, grabs her off the saddle, and his voice detonates across the yard.

"What the hell is wrong with you?"

The words blur after that, swallowed by my own uneven gasps and the hammering of my heartbeat in my ears.

His hands are rough but careful when he finally scoops me up. He smells like sweat and cigarette smoke and the oil he always keeps on his skin from working on engines. I press my face into his shirt and shake.

Over his shoulder, I see the flowerbed—railroad ties knocked out of place, dirt gouged deep, a space where something fragile tried to grow and got trampled instead.

I don't understand all of it yet. I'm six. I know about bikes, and horses, and which cupboard the cereal is in. But a thought settles into me anyway, heavy as a stone in a pond:

She didn't try to stop.

Later, I'll realize it wasn't just that my mother failed to protect me.
It was that, for a moment, she chose not to.

And once you learn your own mother can aim a thousand pounds of animal at you and call it a lesson, you start to understand just how alone you really are.

CHAPTER TWO

Thrown From the Camper

***

Long before the horse ran me down, my mother had already shown me where I ranked on her list of priorities.

I was about three years old the day of the camper.

It sat on the side of the house like an abandoned spaceship—faded white, dented corners, rust nibbling at the edges, weeds curling around its tires. To the grown-ups, it was just a beat-up trailer nobody used anymore.

To me, it was a mountain.

I don't know how I got up there.

A ladder, maybe. A milk crate. A stray cinder block. More likely it was just a moment when no one was watching, and my curiosity found a way.

What I remember is the sky.

One second I was on the ground, and the next I was standing on the roof, the world spread out under my feet. The yard looked small from up there. The grass made patchy patterns. The gravel driveway turned into a gray river. The wind pressed against my bare arms, cool and proud.

I bounced on my little legs, laughing, thrilled by my own daring.

"Mom! Look at me!" I shouted.

In that split second, I believed this would be one of those movie moments. The kind where the mom looks up, hand over her heart, half-scolding but secretly delighted.

Most little kids imagine a mother who will smile and say,
Look at you, you wild thing.

My mother didn't smile.

She turned from whatever she was doing and found me with her eyes. Her mouth flattened into that hard line I would eventually learn to read like a weather report: trouble coming.

"Get down from there," she snapped.

"I can't!" I yelled back.

I giggled, not because I thought it was funny, but because I didn't know what else to do. At three years old, I understood climbing up. I didn't understand climbing down. I just knew I was high and small and suddenly aware of how far the ground was.

What I wanted was help.

What I got was punishment.

My mother marched over to the camper. No rush, no panic, no trembling hands. She stopped below me, narrowed her eyes, and reached up.

She didn't ask me to scoot closer.
She didn't say, "Hang on, I've got you."
She didn't count, "One, two, three."

She just grabbed me—arm, shirt, something—and yanked.

The world dropped out from under my feet.

For a heartbeat, I was weightless. Then gravity slammed me downward. My stomach lurched, my heart punched my ribs, and a scream tore out of my throat.

I didn't land on my feet.
I landed everywhere.

My body hit the ground with a thud that rattled my insides. Pain shot up my side. Rocks and dirt scraped my skin. The breath whooshed out of me so fast there was nothing left to cry with.

Time did that strange stretching thing where a few seconds feel like a whole other life.

I stared up at the sky, little chest struggling to remember how to breathe. The clouds blurred. The edges of the world went soft and white around my vision.

For a moment, I wondered if this was what dying felt like small and stunned and strangely quiet.

My mother didn't bend down to see if I was okay.

She didn't check for broken bones.
She didn't ask if I could move.
She didn't say my name.

She turned and walked away.

Just like that. Problem handled. Camper cleared. Child still breathing? Not her concern.

It was my older sisters my dad's daughters from his first marriage who rushed in. They were taller versions of me, similar faces stretching over wide, worried eyes.

"Are you okay?" one of them asked, dropping to her knees beside me.

"Can you move?" another said, her hand hovering near my arm but not quite touching, like I might shatter if she did.

I wanted to sob. My throat burned with it. My body ached in ways I didn't have words for yet.

But even at three, I already knew the rules.

Crying meant you were weak.
Weakness made people angry.
Anger turned into pain.

So I swallowed the cry and dragged myself upright, every muscle protesting. Gravel stuck to my palms. My knees stung. My head felt too light.

"I'm fine," I croaked.

They didn't believe me, not really. Their hands stayed close, ready in case I tipped over. Their faces were tight with the kind of fear you get when you watch something awful happen and realize no one in charge thinks it's a problem.

Behind the house, my mother's footsteps faded away like an afterthought.

Later, I'd file that memory under a pattern: how quickly she walked away from me, again and again and again.

But at three, all I had was confusion.

If the person who's supposed to catch you throws you instead, who are you supposed to trust?

I didn't know it then, sitting there in the dirt and pain, but a few years later I'd find out just how far a

father could go in the opposite direction—
catching me, cheering me on…
    …and still bringing danger right to my feet.

CHAPTER THREE

A Room Full of Trophies

***

*I*f my mother made me feel small and unwanted, my father made me feel like I was built out of something powerful even if that "something" wasn't always safe.

By the time I was four or five, our house had its own shrine.

We called it the trophy room.

Shelves lined the walls, sagging under the weight of gold-colored plastic men frozen mid-stride, mid-leap, mid-race. Snowmobiles carved from cheap metal rode eternal waves of fake snow across wooden bases. The room smelled like old cigarettes, cold dust, and motor oil embedded in every surface.

My dad raced anything with an engine.

Snowmobiles in the winter, dirt bikes or sleds, whatever would move fast and loud under him. He raced for Budweiser, for bragging rights, for the rush that lit him up from the inside out. At the tracks and on the ice, he wasn't just some guy.

He was *Ray*—a name people knew.

Wherever he went, he took me with him.

The races felt like another planet. Engines screamed. The air snapped cold against my cheeks. Snow and ice sprayed up in glittering arcs as machines tore past. Men shouted and laughed over the noise, their breath ghosting in the freezing air. Women huddled together in thick jackets, boots planted in the snow, cups of coffee or beer warming their hands.

I didn't sit on the sidelines.

I worked my version of it.

I marched around with a black trash bag, collecting pop cans and bottles people tossed aside. My small gloved hands grabbed whatever lay near the snowbanks—aluminum, cups, stray trash. Every can that clinked into my bag felt like proof.

Proof that I belonged.
Proof that I was part of this world, not just tagging along.

"Ray's kid," people would say as I walked by.

"That one's tough."

The words warmed me more than my coat ever could.

At home, I was the problem. The too-loud, too-clumsy, too-much girl who got run over in flowerbeds and thrown from campers.

At the races, I was part of the team.

One year around 1977, when I was three going on four, my dad's friend Tony called us over behind the house. The snow had started to recede into dirty piles along the fence. The air smelled like melting ice and gasoline.

Tony grinned and rolled something out from the garage.

It was the most beautiful thing I'd ever seen: a small red Honda three-wheeler, metal gleaming, seat black and perfect, handlebars wide and waiting.

It looked like a machine built just for me.

They rolled it out like a prize from the trophy room itself.

"You think you can handle this?" Tony asked, smirking, eyebrows up.

I was tiny. The handlebars were practically at eye level.

But I puffed up my chest and nodded. "Yeah."

My dad watched me with that half-amused, half-proud look he got when I did something reckless he secretly respected. He started explaining the basics—the throttle, the brake, where my feet should go—but his words blurred into a humming backdrop.

My heart pounded louder than his voice.
All I could think was: *I get one. I get my own.*

They set me on the seat.

The world shrank to the hum of the engine and the feel of the grips in my hands. My fingers tingled. The machine vibrated under me, alive and humming, waiting to see who I was going to be.

"Easy on the throttle," my dad said. "Just a little at a time."

I nodded like I understood.

I did not understand.

I did what kids do when handed something powerful for the first time.

I went all the way.

The second I twisted my wrist, the engine roared like it had been waiting years for that moment. The three-wheeler shot forward. The yard became a blur of color and cold air. My eyes watered. Adrenaline exploded through my tiny body.

For a few wild seconds, I was flying.

Then the machine met the laws of physics and lost.

I hit something maybe a rut, maybe a hidden rock, maybe just the edge of the driveway and the three-wheeler kicked sideways. The world tilted. The handlebars jerked out of my hands.

I was airborne again, just like off the camper, only this time the speed was my idea.

I hit the ground and rolled. Snow, ice, dirt, sky everything became a tumbling mess of color and impact. My elbow smashed into something hard. My hip lit up with pain.

Then I stopped.

Silence rang in my ears, empty and strange after the roar.

I lay there, staring up at the sky, stunned and breathless. For a moment, I didn't know if I was hurt or just shocked. Everything felt bruised. Everything felt far away.

Then I realized I could move my fingers. My toes. My jaw.

I let out a shaky sound. It was supposed to be a sob. It turned into a laugh.

A wild, breathless, half-hysterical laugh.

I rolled onto my side and pushed myself up, body trembling. Across the yard, the three-wheeler was a broken heap. The frame had snapped, the front twisted at an angle no machine was designed to survive.

I stared at it, waiting.

Not for help.

For consequences.

I braced for my father's rage for the yelling, the cussing, the slap, the look that said I had ruined everything. Years of living with my mother had trained me well: breaking things usually meant punishment.

Instead, I heard something I didn't expect.

My father laughed.

"Kid broke the damn frame," he said to Tony, eyes wide in a mix of shock and pride. "She ain't scared of anything."

The pride in his voice landed in me like sunlight.

I was still aching, still shaking, but in that second, I didn't feel like the girl who got thrown from campers and left in the dirt. I didn't feel like the kid my mother walked away from without a backward glance.

I felt tough.

Fearless.

His.

I didn't understand yet how twisted that was—that I was learning to measure my worth by how much pain I could take without crying.

I didn't realize yet that the same man who stood there bragging about me, laughing at my crash, was also a man people whispered about in corners and in back rooms.

The trophies kept piling up on the shelves.

So did the stories.

And while he shined those gold plastic statues and brought me along like a sidekick, he was also taking me into darker places—rooms with plastic on the walls and secrets in the air.

Places where I would start to understand that being proud of my father and being afraid of him could exist in the same breath.

CHAPTER FOUR

Shadows of the Underground

***

By the time I was eight, I knew there were two versions of my father.

There was the racer the man people cheered for, the man whose name rolled over loudspeakers at winter tracks and summer fields. The man who grinned with a cigarette in his teeth, helmet under his arm, trophy in his hand, my small gloved hand wrapped in his free one.

And there was the other one.

The man who disappeared at odd hours.
The man neighbors talked about in half-finished sentences.
The man whose favors weren't the kind you ever put in writing.

One night, he took me to a house I'd never seen before.

We drove in the dark, the truck headlights cutting tunnels through the black. No radio, no idle chatter. Just the low rumble of the engine and the occasional flick of his hand to tap ash out the cracked window.

The house we pulled up to looked ordinary enough from the street.

Plain yard. No toys. No swing set. No garden. Just a square of grass, a porch light burning a weak pool of yellow against the night.

But the air felt wrong.

Thick. Tight. Like the world was holding its breath.

Inside, the first thing I noticed was the plastic.

Clear sheets hung along the lower parts of the walls, taped in place, crinkling when anyone brushed too close. More plastic draped over some of the furniture, leaving the shapes underneath ghostly and strange.

It looked like someone was expecting a mess and didn't want it to stick.

Men stood against the walls and in doorways. They didn't talk much. They watched. Their faces were blank in that deliberate way grown-ups sometimes wear when they don't want kids to know what they're thinking.

No one told me to go outside.
No one said, "She shouldn't be here."

So I stayed.

I stood close to my father, my small hand hovering a few inches from his jacket, not quite touching. My heart thudded against my ribs, loud in my own ears.

Someone was kneeling in the middle of the room.

Their shoulders were hunched. Their head was bowed. I couldn't see their face clearly, but what I felt from them wasn't the kind of fear I'd seen at the racetrack or during fights at home.

This was different.

Colder.

Resigned.

Like they were waiting for something they already knew was coming.

My dad's friend stepped forward and handed him something.

I didn't need to see exactly what it was. I just knew the weight of the room changed. The air sharpened. The men leaning against the walls seemed to lean in without moving at all.

My father took it, whatever it was, and the child part of me understood something without language:

My dad could be the man people cheered for…

…and he could be the man people were afraid of.

I don't remember many words after that. Sounds blurred together the low murmur of voices, the rustle of plastic, a noise that made my skin crawl and my stomach twist without understanding why.

What stuck with me wasn't a single action.

It was the calm.

Nobody panicked.

Nobody protested.

Nobody rushed to stop anything.

It was all so organized, so quiet, like this was just another task on a list of things grown men did on weeknights.

When we finally stepped back out into the night, the yard felt colder than it had when we arrived.

The stars looked sharper, like broken glass scattered across the sky.

The air tasted like secrets.

My father didn't explain.

He didn't say, "Don't tell your mother."
He didn't say, "You didn't see anything."

He just walked to the truck, climbed in, and started the engine like we were leaving a grocery store instead of a room wrapped in plastic.

I climbed in beside him, the seat rough under my palms. The dashboard lights painted his face in harsh angles—cheekbones catching green, eyes shadowed, mouth a tight line.

We drove in silence.

I pressed my forehead to the cold window and watched the dark fields slide by, broken only by the occasional lonely streetlight casting sickly halos on the road.

I felt older than I had that morning.

Not taller.
Not wiser.

Just heavier.

I had already learned that my mother could hurt me and walk away like it was nothing—that she could throw me from heights and run me down and still sleep just fine afterward.

Now I was learning that my father could hurt other people in ways I didn't have names for yet.

And the scariest part wasn't even what I saw.

It was how normal it seemed to everyone else in that room.

Like this was just…what happened. Like violence was a job. Like danger was a tool you picked up and put down when you needed it.

We pulled into our driveway, the house dark except for a thin line of light under a curtain. My father killed the engine, flicked his cigarette butt into the gravel, and sat for a second, staring straight ahead.

Then he got out and went inside.

No lecture. No warning. No comfort.

Just the same quiet man with two lives, slipping from one into the other.

I followed him, little footsteps echoing in the hallway, heart still thudding from things I didn't understand.

At home, the danger didn't always wear plastic or quiet faces.

Sometimes it came with screaming, breaking things, and a knife pulled in the middle of a Sunday morning, and I was about to find out what it felt like when that kind of storm exploded in the middle of our kitchen.

CHAPTER FIVE

The Fire

***

If my dad's world was engines and shadows, my mother's world was tight control and a rage she kept on a low boil.

Before the big Victorian house, we lived in a smaller place—walls thin as a secret, floors that groaned when you walked across them, heat that seemed to leak out through every crack. The furnace always smelled a little like burned dust and oil. The kitchen was narrow, the kind of space where if one person turned around too fast, everyone else had to move.

That was the backdrop for one of the few pure memories of joy I had back then: a road trip to Kings Island when I was about seven.

We went on bikes and trailers and whatever else my dad could get moving down the highway. There were rides and crowds and noise and all the things kids are supposed to remember when they grow up.

What stuck with me wasn't any of that.

It was potato wedges.

We were sitting at some park restaurant, fluorescent lights buzzing overhead, the air full of fryer grease and chatter. A red plastic basket landed in front of me, lined with paper, piled with thick wedges of potato—crispy on the outside, soft on the inside, dusted with some kind of seasoning that tasted like everything good at once.

I picked one up with my little fingers, blew on the steam, took a bite, and for a few seconds nothing else existed.

Not yelling.
Not fear.
Not the feeling that at any moment someone might explode over something I didn't understand.

Just salt and crunch and heat and the simple miracle of something made just to be enjoyed.

Those stupid wedges carved out a space in my memory and stayed there.

After we got home, the house still held that faint, stale smell of smoke from the furnace, the walls worn and dingy. The trip began to fade around the edges like dreams do.

But the potatoes didn't.

"Dad," I said one day, standing in the kitchen with my chin just above the counter. "I want those Kings Island potato wedges."

He looked at me for a second, something unreadable passing through his eyes. Maybe he saw a chance to give me something good. Maybe he'd been thinking about those wedges too. Maybe he just liked a challenge.

"Alright," he said. "Let's make 'em."

He said it like it was simple. Like all the complicated, dangerous parts of our life could pause long enough for oil and potatoes.

He pulled out a big pot, set it on the gas stove, and filled it with oil. The blue flames beneath licked at the metal until the surface shimmered, catching the kitchen light in uneasy waves.

I watched from a chair he'd dragged over for me. At seven, I was big enough to "help" but small enough that everything I did still required climbing on something.

He washed the potatoes in the sink, the water running loud and cold over his hands. He sliced them into thick wedges, dropped them in a metal bowl, and set it beside me. They glistened with a thin coat of water, little droplets clinging stubbornly to the sides.

"When I tell you, you dump them in," he said, nodding toward the pot.

My small hands curled around the bowl. The burner hissed quietly under the oil. The kitchen felt smaller than usual, full of heat and expectation.

I wanted so badly to get it right.

To be part of this.

To help make the thing that had made me feel so happy.

My dad watched the oil, testing it with a bit of potato, waiting for the sizzle he wanted.

"Now," he said.

I tipped the bowl.

The instant the wet potatoes hit that pot, the world turned violent.

Oil exploded upward with a furious hiss, like the stove had been waiting for a chance to attack.

Grease sprayed into the air, spattering the burner, the walls, the underside of the cabinets. Flames leapt up out of the pot, grabbed the oily splash on the back wall, and raced up it like they'd been given a map.

Fire roared to life in front of my face.

The heat hit me so hard it felt like a slap. I stumbled backward on the chair, arms pinwheeling. My heart hammered in my throat, too big for my small chest.

"Get back!" my dad yelled.

He lunged between me and the flames, grabbing a towel, trying to smother the fire. But every movement seemed to feed it. The flames clawed at the wall, tasting paint and old grease, reaching higher, brighter, louder.

For a handful of seconds, I thought:

We're going to burn the whole house down. We're going to die because I asked for potato wedges.

My mother appeared in the doorway.

For that fraction of a moment, I thought I saw concern on her face like maybe she'd rush forward, pull me back, grab a lid or a blanket, do something, anything, to help put out the fire.

But the concern—if it was ever there—flickered out fast.

What took its place was fury.

Not fear for her children. Not panic over the flames clawing at her kitchen.

Anger.

At him.

At me.

At the black marks already forming on her wall.

Somehow, between my dad's frantic smothering and the fire finally strangling itself out of fuel, the flames went down. Smoke filled the kitchen, thick and bitter. My eyes watered, my throat burned, my lungs clawed for air. My hands shook so hard I had to hold onto the back of the chair to keep from falling.

The wall behind the stove was scorched, an ugly black-and-brown wound up the back of the oven and over the cabinets. Splashes of oil left shiny, dirty arcs that would never quite wash off.

I stared at it, trembling, my body still buzzing with leftover adrenaline.

I wanted someone to say, *Are you okay?*

I wanted someone to laugh and say, *Well, that didn't work,* and then hug me until the shaking stopped.

Nobody did.

What they said later was something else entirely.

The story of that day started simple: Dad had an idea, I helped, the oil was too hot, the potatoes were too wet, and we had a grease fire.

But by the time it passed through my mother's mouth enough times, it changed shape.

It wasn't "We tried to make fries and it went bad."

It wasn't "He told her to dump the potatoes and the oil flashed."

It became:

"Lena burned the house down."

She said it with this bitter little twist in her voice, like she took satisfaction in it. Like me ruining things fit into some story she'd already decided about who I was.

The girl who couldn't do anything right.
The girl who broke things.
The girl who was always to blame.

Nobody mentioned that it was my father's idea.
Nobody mentioned that I was seven.
Nobody mentioned that I had done exactly what I was told.

Just "Lena burned the house down," over and over, until even I started to feel like maybe I really had flames in my hands.

The wall behind the stove stayed stained long after the smoke cleared. It wasn't just burn marks and grease.

It was a reminder of the version of me my mother chose to believe in:

The girl who set everything on fire.

And if I wasn't starting fires, I was still somehow the problem—
even on the day my father pressed a knife between us and promised to cut our throats if we ran.

CHAPTER SIX

Never a Family, Only a Fight

***

The older I got, the more I understood that
what other people called "family," we lived as a war
zone.

My parents didn't drink.
They didn't have pills to blame.
They fought like that stone-cold sober.

Around 1979 to 1981, when I was about seven,
we were living in a tired little place off a dirt road.
It was the kind of house that felt like it was exhaling
all the time—windows drafty, floors slanting just
enough that toys rolled on their own, stairs that
complained with every step.

Our bedroom was up in the attic, my sister and
I. You reached it by pulling down a fold-out ladder
from the ceiling. It creaked and wobbled and
smelled like dry wood and dust, but to us it meant
we had a space that was ours, even if the roof
leaned in too close.

One Sunday morning, the neighbors offered to
take us to Sunday school.

It felt like being invited into some other world—
the kind where people went to church and had
potlucks afterward and took family pictures where

nobody had a black eye or a hole in the wall behind them.

My mother had sewn matching dresses for us. Nothing fancy, but to me they might as well have been ball gowns. Soft fabric, little hems she'd ironed herself, stitches small and neat. I stood in the attic bedroom, the ladder open like a doorway to something normal below, smoothing my hands over the front of the dress.

For a few heartbeats, I felt like any other little girl.

Church dress.
Sunday morning.
The promise of coloring pages and songs about Jesus loving children.

We started down the fold-out ladder, careful not to slip. My hand slid along the cool metal side rail, my shoes thumping on each rung.

The moment we reached the bottom, the illusion shattered.

My parents were already fighting.

Their voices crashed into each other my mother's high and sharp, my father's low and booming. The air felt thick, like their anger had used up most of the oxygen. The neighbors' car idled outside, waiting politely, as if they had no idea a storm was breaking inside.

In the living room, my father grabbed the VCR—a gold-colored, heavy thing, the kind of appliance most people would handle carefully because it cost more than anything else in the room.

He didn't handle it carefully.

He hurled it across the room.

It smashed into the wall with a sickening, metallic crunch, pieces flying, plastic and wiring and circuits raining down. For a second, it looked like the wall itself had shattered.

My heart slammed against my ribs. The dress that had made me feel special a minute ago suddenly felt like a costume in the wrong play.

My sister and I moved as one toward the front door, drawn to the idea of escape of the quiet car, of church, of any place where voices didn't sound like weapons.

We didn't make it.

In the space between the broken VCR hitting the floor and the neighbors stepping onto our porch, everything escalated.

My dad pinned my mother against the wall.

His hand clamped around her arm, fingers digging in so tight the skin blanched beneath them. His face was inches from hers, jaw clenched so hard I thought his teeth might crack. Her eyes flashed, but there was a flicker of something else there too— real fear cutting through the rage.

The room telescoped.

The edges of my vision went soft. The only sharp thing left was the image of my father's hand reaching to his belt, pulling something free.

A knife.

He flipped it open with a practiced flick, the blade catching the weak morning light that slanted through the window.

The house went quiet in my head.

I could still see my mother's lips moving. I could see my sister's eyes, wide and glassy. I knew outside, the neighbors were probably sitting in their car checking their watch, wondering what was taking us so long.

But inside that room, everything narrowed to the point of that blade.

"If you run," my father said.

His voice wasn't loud. It wasn't a shout. It was worse steady, low, as sure as gravity.

He looked at my mother first, then at us.

"If you run, I will catch you. And I will slice your throats."

The words dropped into the room like stones into water.

He didn't need to raise his voice.
He didn't need to repeat himself.

The promise in the way he said it made my skin crawl.

Every muscle in my body screamed to move. To grab my sister's hand, to bolt for the door, to sprint across the yard and fling myself into the neighbors' car and refuse to ever come back.

But my legs wouldn't listen.

It felt like someone had poured concrete into my feet. My knees locked. My fingers dug into the skirt of my dress until the fabric wrinkled under my fists.

We didn't run.

We didn't even breathe loud.

The front door might as well have been a thousand miles away.

In that moment, the idea of "escape" rearranged itself in my seven-year-old brain. It stopped being something you could just *do*. It became something dangerous, something that might end with a blade against your skin.

Eventually, the moment broke.

I don't remember what words came next. More yelling, probably. Maybe my mother backing down. Maybe my father storming outside. Maybe the neighbors driving away when we didn't come out, deciding church could wait.

What I remember is the weight that settled inside me after:

If the people who are supposed to protect you are the ones you're afraid of,
where exactly are you supposed to run?

I smoothed my dress after the fight, straightened the hem like I could iron the morning flat again with my hands.

We didn't make it to Sunday school.

We stayed in that house, in that war, walking around the knife-shaped hole in the air like it was just another piece of furniture.

For years, I thought that was just how families were—
violence pressed up against the everyday, threats mixed in with breakfast and church invitations.

I didn't know that soon enough, the danger would stop threatening and start flying through the air in a straight line, aimed right at the window behind my back.

PART II

THE HOME THAT WAS NEVER HOME

CHAPTER SEVEN

The Night the Shot Came Through the Window

***

*B*y the time I was eight, danger didn't surprise me much anymore.

It was like the wallpaper in our lives—always there, whether anyone pointed it out or not.

We were still in that little house on the dirt road then—the one with the slanted floors and the couch pressed right up against the front window. Outside, the road was mostly dust and gravel. When trucks went by, they threw up clouds that took forever to settle. You could hear the occasional car long before you saw its headlights sweep past.

Inside, everything smelled faintly of smoke and old grease and the ghosts of a hundred burned dinners.

The TV sat kitty-corner near the window, rabbit ears stretched out like they were reaching for a better life. The couch backed right up to the glass, the cushions worn into familiar grooves by all the times I'd flopped down with cartoons or static-filled movies.

One night, I was sitting there with my legs tucked under me, eyes on the screen. The glow flickered across the glass inches from the back of my head. My hair brushed the cold windowpane whenever I shifted.

My dad sat at the bar that separated the kitchen from the living room, perched on a stool like it was his throne. Next to him was his friend Bobby, a man I knew by the worn flannel shirts and the way he always seemed half-amused by everything.

They talked the way grown men talk when they think kids aren't really listening—low voices, half-finished sentences, names I didn't recognize. The clink of a glass. The low, rough sound of my dad's laugh.

In the background: the hum of the refrigerator. The faint rattle of the furnace kicking on. The TV doing its best to drown the house in someone else's story.

I remember the weight of the window at my back.

I remember thinking, for once, that things were…if not calm, at least familiar.

Then came a sound that did not belong.

A sharp *pop*.

Louder than a hand clap, quieter than a firework, but wrong in a way that made my whole body tense before my mind had time to form the word *gun*.

The window behind me exploded.

Glass shattered around my shoulders in an instant, raining down in glittering shards. Tiny knives of glass nicked my skin, tangled in my hair, slid down the back of my neck. For a second I didn't move, stunned by the shock of air rushing in where solid glass had been a heartbeat before.

Then Bobby fell.

One moment he was a man sitting on a barstool, talking to my father. The next, he was sliding off, his body folding in on itself like a puppet with the strings cut. He hit the floor in a crumpled heap of flannel and denim.

The world shrank to sounds:

The TV still playing, oblivious.

My heart pounding so loud it felt like the only noise in the room.

My dad's chair scraping back hard against the floor.

He was already moving before I could turn.

He bolted for the door, shoulders tight, jaw set. The front yard flooded with light as someone's headlights swept across it. I could see the outline of a car at the edge of our property, the engine still running, exhaust curling into the night.

My father didn't stop to ask questions.

He went straight for the driver's side, reached through the open window, and grabbed the man inside.

There was no slow build, no hesitation.

He just yanked him halfway out of the car and started swinging.

His fists landed with the kind of force that comes from someone who's already stared death in the face and decided he'd rather be the one doing the hitting. The man in the car flailed, trapped between the seatbelt and my father's grip. The sounds were messy thuds and grunts and the scrape of denim on metal.

Inside, Bobby lay on the floor.

Someone maybe another man, maybe my mother was shouting. There was blood. There was always blood, it seemed, whenever my father's two worlds collided like this.

Then everything smeared into Mayhem.

Sirens.

Red and blue lights bouncing off the front of the house, turning our dirty siding into something out of a crime show. Strangers in uniforms stepping over broken glass, asking questions with tight faces.

Neighbors peered from behind curtains. Some came out and stood on the edges of the yard, arms folded against the cold, eyes wide and hungry for drama.

I stood there with tiny bits of glass still clinging to my hair, the couch behind me torn open by the bullet, foam peeking through the ripped fabric.

No one wrapped a blanket around my shoulders. No one sat me down and checked my skin for cuts. No one knelt to look me in the eyes and say, *That was scary. You're okay. I've got you.*

I swept the couch off myself, tiny clear daggers biting into my palms as I brushed them away. My fingers stung. My chest still buzzed with leftover fear.

At some point, the car was hauled off. The shooter was taken wherever shooters go. Bobby was taken wherever bleeding men go. The sirens faded.

Later, my dad came home.

His clothes were muddy, his boots soaked and caked like he'd gone through more than just our front yard. Behind him, other men pulled up—his people, the ones who came when there was trouble, their faces set and serious.

They stood in our yard and talked in low voices like this was a meeting instead of the aftermath of someone trying to kill us.

For a long time, I told myself a simple story:

He defended us.

He fought for us.

He went after the man who shot into our house, who could have killed me or Bobby or anyone else in that room.

And that was true.

But it was only half.

The other half, the part I didn't have the words for yet, was this:

If bullets are flying through your living room window, if men are pulling up ready for war, if a child is sweeping glass off the couch by herself while adults talk business in the yard—

then your life is not safe, no matter how hard your father swings his fists.

The couch got replaced eventually. The window got fixed. The glass disappeared from the carpet and the cushions.

But the night the shot came through the window stayed with me.

Another reminder that in our house, danger
didn't just live in the threats and fights and knives
held too close.

Sometimes, it came from outside...
aiming straight for us.

And the worst part was knowing:

We were the kind of family people shot at.

CHAPTER EIGHT

The Victorian House

***

When people hear "Victorian house," they picture something out of a postcard gingerbread trim, tall ceilings, wraparound porch, stained glass catching the sun.

From the road, ours almost passed for that. By then, I was around eight, already old enough to know that a pretty house didn't mean a safe one.

It sat back off the main street at the end of a long, rutted driveway, big and tired and watching. Two stories of peeling paint and sagging roofline, narrow windows like half-lidded eyes. The porch leaned a little, as if the whole place had exhaled one long, exhausted sigh and never quite pulled itself upright again.

The first time we pulled in, gravel popping under the tires, I remember thinking the house looked… aware. Like it had seen things and wasn't impressed we were adding to them.

Inside, the air was cool and faintly damp, with that old-house smell dust, wood, something sour deep in the walls that no amount of cleaning ever really erased. The floors complained with every step, boards creaking in long, slow groans that traveled down the hallway ahead of you, warning the house you were coming.

Everyone said the basement was haunted.

"It was on the Underground Railroad," someone told me, like they were bragging. "There are tunnels underneath. You can still hear them sometimes."

Them. The people who had hidden here. The people who'd waited in the dark, listening for footsteps above their heads and wondering if this house would keep them alive or get them caught.

As a kid, the story crawled under my skin and stayed there.

Sometimes I'd stand at the top of the basement stairs, hand on the rail, breathing in that dirt-heavy air. The shadows pooled thick at the bottom of the steps, deeper than they should have been. If I stood there long enough, my mind would start filling in sounds that might've been nothing: a faint shift, the scrape of something on stone, a sigh.

I'd picture families curled together in the dark—mothers holding their children tight, men pressed against cold walls, every ear tuned to the floorboards above. Listening the way I lay in bed and listened for my parents' voices coming up through the vents.

Freedom upstairs for them. Hell upstairs for me.

The house was big, but there wasn't much room that really belonged to me. My bedroom was tucked under the eaves on the second floor, a long, narrow space with sloped ceiling and worn carpet, like someone had stretched a hallway into a bedroom and then changed their mind halfway through.

One whole wall was almost entirely glass.

Once, there had been a balcony there. You could see the old brackets still bolted into the siding outside, rusted metal hands reaching for something that wasn't there anymore. Now it was just a sliding glass door opening onto a drop—nothing but thin air and the hard ground two stories below.

A door to nowhere.

During the day, light poured through that glass like a spotlight. At night, it turned into a black mirror. My own reflection hovered there over the darkness outside, superimposed on whatever might be moving beyond the yard.

I'd stand in front of it, toes against the metal track, forehead resting lightly on the cool pane. From that angle, if I squinted, it almost looked like the missing balcony was still there, just invisible. Like maybe if I slid the door open and stepped out, solid boards would appear under my feet.

Part of me knew better.

Another part of me wondered what it would feel like to just… take one more step.

I didn't have words like suicide or depression. I didn't know phrases like intrusive thoughts. All I knew was that sometimes, when my mother's voice rose downstairs and my father's anger collided with hers and the house filled up with the sound of them ripping each other apart, that glass looked less like a safety barrier and more like an answer.

If I disappeared, would they stop?

If I vanished into the air beyond that door, would the yelling finally go with me?

I never opened it. Not all the way.

But I thought about it.

At night, when I crawled into bed, the glass loomed at the edge of my vision. The house made its noises floorboards shifting, old beams popping as the temperature changed, the distant hum of pipes—and every sound felt like someone else breathing in the dark.

Sometimes it was just the house settling.

Sometimes it was my parents, still up, still fighting, their voices rising through vents and thin walls. Words blurred into shapes—accusation, threats, curses that didn't need details to land. I'd lie there, eyes locked on that door, wondering which would crack first: the glass, or me.

Down the hall from my room was another space that didn't quite know what it wanted to be. A long, unfinished room stretched the length of the house, narrow and low, with bare floorboards and exposed beams like ribs. It smelled like dry wood, old insulation, and forgotten summers.

Light slipped in from small, grimy windows at either end, cutting the darkness into slivers. Boxes were stacked along the walls, half-collapsed cardboard full of things no one cared enough to unpack. Out-of-season clothes. Broken toys. A lamp with no shade. The leftovers of other lives we'd already torn through.

That room felt like a secret all by itself.

I'd walk it end to end sometimes, my footsteps soft, the boards hollow under my feet. At one end, there was a narrow gap where I could look down at the road and the curve of the driveway— a tiny slice of the world beyond our walls. At the other end, there was only trees and nowhere else to go and neighbors' roofs, the lives of people who probably slept through the night without counting exits. I didn't know yet that I would need that long room. That it would become a hiding place. A place to press myself into the angles of the house and listen for danger passing by.

All I knew was that the house felt alive in a way our smaller ones never had.

They'd been cages.

This one was a creature—bones and breath and memory. It held the echo of other people's terror and other people's bravery, layered under our shouting and slammed doors, like sediment in a riverbed.

The adults talked about how lucky we were.

"Bigger place," my father said, eyes scanning the yard like it was something he'd conquered. "More room. Nice house."

My mother moved through it like she was walking through someone else's bad dream, jaw tight, shoulders sharp. She knew how to turn a compliment into a complaint in three seconds flat. The paint was wrong. The neighbors were nosy. The windows leaked. The bills were too high.

Nothing was ever enough for her.

Not this house.

Not my dad.

Definitely not me.

At school, kids would say, "Oh, you live in that big old house on the corner? That place is so cool." Their voices carried this breathless fascination, like they were picturing chandeliers and secret staircases, not police lights reflecting in tall windows at midnight.

I'd shrug.

"Yeah," I'd say. "It's… a house."

I didn't have the language to explain that the walls you live in can be haunted even if there are no ghosts. That a house can be beautiful and still be the worst place you've ever tried to sleep.

So I let them keep their fantasies.

At night, lying there with the glass door at my side and the long, unfinished room down the hall, I listened.

To the creaks under my bed that might have been old beams or might have been something older.

To the low rumble of my father's voice when he was on the phone late, talking business he never explained.

To the sharp, cutting edge of my mother's words when she was tired or wired or just done pretending she liked any of us.

The Victorian house was supposed to be a fresh start.

New town. New neighbors. Bigger rooms. Longer driveway between us and the rest of the world.

But we were the same people.

The same fights moved in with us, just louder in bigger spaces. The same fear unpacked itself in every room I tried to call mine. The same feeling sat heavy on my chest when I woke up and when I went to sleep:

You are not safe here.

And still, some small part of me hoped.

Hoped that maybe in a house this big, there'd be a corner nobody yelled in. A stair I could sit on where no one thought to look for me. A night where the only thing that woke me was the wind pushing against the old windows, and not my mother's footsteps or my father's fury.

I didn't know it yet, but the house wasn't done with us.

Before long, it would hold the worst night of my childhood—my mother naked and screaming, my sister telling me I deserved to die, and police pounding on that front door like they were trying to wake the dead.

CHAPTER NINE

The Night Everything Came Apart

***

In the Victorian house, there were two kinds of nights.

Most were bad in the usual ways—raised voices, slammed doors, my mother's sharp words flung down the stairs like knives, my father's anger answering back. The kind of pandemonium I could almost predict by the sound of the first slammed cabinet.

And then there was *that* night.

The one that split my childhood into a before and after.

I was nine, maybe ten. Old enough to know what "crazy" meant in other people's families. Young enough to still be surprised by just how far mine could go.

The house was already humming with tension by late afternoon.

Drawers banged. Doors shut too hard. My mother's footsteps thudded across the floorboards in quick, angry bursts, like she was searching for something to throw that would feel satisfying enough.

From my room, I could hear her talking to herself.

Not loud, not all at once. Just little fragments drifting up through the vents:

"…sick of this…"

"…they don't appreciate…"

"…see what happens…"

The light outside slid from gold to gray. Shadows lengthened in that long hallway upstairs. The sliding glass door in my room turned from a bright pane to a dark mirror, reflecting my own anxious pacing back at me.

I tried to stay small.

Feet tucked up on my bed. Back pressed to the wall. A book open in my lap that I wasn't really reading. My ears stretched toward the sounds downstairs.

Then the noises changed.

It wasn't just stomping and muttering anymore. There was a crash sharp, shattering, the unmistakable sound of something glass meeting a wall and losing. Then another. Something heavy toppled. My mother's voice shot up, words ragged and cracked.

"YOU THINK I WON'T? YOU THINK I WON'T DO IT?"

My stomach dropped.

I slid off the bed and padded to my door, bare feet silent on the worn carpet. The hallway beyond was dim, only a sliver of light leaking from the bathroom down the way. The house felt like it was holding its breath.

My sister appeared from her room, face pale, eyes too wide.

"What's happening?" I whispered.

She shook her head once, sharp. "You know what's happening."

And I did.

I'd seen pieces of it before—my mother's moods stretching too tight, snapping in ways that never made sense, the threats, the way she used her own life as a bargaining chip she never quite cashed in.

But this time felt different.

Bigger.

Louder.

Like something ugly had finally grown too large to stay inside her skin.

We edged to the top of the stairs and looked down through the railing.

The living room was tipped on its side.

Couch cushions flung across the floor. A lamp shattered, its shade crushed underfoot. A picture frame lay face down, glass splintered, the smiling photo inside smeared with something dark—I hoped it was just spilled coffee.

And in the center of it all:

My mother.

Naked.

She paced in jagged lines, hair wild, skin flushed an angry, blotchy red. Her eyes were blown wide, pupils too big, whites showing all the way around like a cornered animal's. She clutched something in her hand a knife, maybe, or a shard of glass; I couldn't quite see from where I stood, heart pounding so loud it made the edges of my vision pulse.

"Go ahead!" she screamed toward the front door, toward the windows, toward the world. "CALL THEM! I DON'T CARE! I DON'T CARE ANYMORE!"

Her voice cracked on the last word, tearing into a sound that wasn't quite a scream and wasn't quite a sob. It was something worse—like grief and rage had mixed together and come out wrong.

My father stood off to the side, jaw clenched, hands open at his sides like he couldn't decide whether to grab her or let her go.

"Marjorie," he said—using her name in that low, warning tone. "Put it down. Quit actin' like this."

She whirled on him.

"You did this!" she spat. "You and *them*."

She flung an arm in the general direction of the stairs. Of us.

I ducked back instinctively, pressing my spine to the wall, breath shallow. My sister stayed where she was, fingers gripping the banister so tight her knuckles went white. Her jaw was clenched so hard the muscles jumped in her cheek.

"Don't come down here," she hissed over her shoulder. "Just stay put, Lena."

But I could still see through the gaps in the railing.

My mother stalked toward the kitchen, bare feet crunching over broken glass. Every step tracked a smear of something—spilled liquid, dirt, maybe blood. She yanked a drawer open so hard it came off the track, silverware scattering.

"THIS IS WHAT YOU WANTED!" she shouted to no one and everyone at once. "YOU WANT ME GONE? I'LL GO! I'LL GO FOR GOOD!"

There was a flurry of movement—my father trying to get closer without setting her off further, my mother jerking away, shrieking threats. She was talking about killing herself. About making sure everybody "remembered what they'd done" when she did it.

Somewhere in all of that, someone called the cops.

Maybe it was a neighbor, finally fed up with the sounds pouring out of our windows. Maybe it was my dad in a moment of fear, choosing sirens over the image of her actually following through this time. Maybe it was my sister, fingers shaking around the phone.

What I know is the pounding came next.

Fists on the front door, loud enough to rattle the frame.

"POLICE! OPEN UP!"

My mother went very still.

For a single frozen heartbeat, the whole house held its breath with her.

Then she screamed.

Not words at first. Just raw sound. She spun toward the door, naked and shaking, knife or glass still in her hand. For a second I thought she would charge it, hurl herself at the wood and whoever waited on the other side.

My sister's hand shot out, grabbing my wrist through the railing.

"This is your fault," she whispered, voice harsh and shaking. "You know that, right?"

Her nails dug into my skin.

"If you weren't such a problem, if you didn't make everything worse, she wouldn't be like this. You *deserve* to die."

The words punched through me harder than any fist.

I felt them more than I heard them—like they slipped under my ribs and settled there, heavy and sharp.

I didn't argue.

I didn't say, *I'm nine.*

I didn't say, *I didn't ask for any of this.*

I didn't say, *You're wrong.*

Instead, I believed her.

Of course it was my fault. I was the camper kid, the grease-fire kid, the girl who "burned the house down," the one who got run over and still somehow ended up blamed for standing in the wrong place.

Why wouldn't this be my fault too?

The pounding on the door came again.

"POLICE! OPEN THE DOOR!"

My father moved fast then, crossing the wrecked living room in three strides. My mother screamed something about not letting them in, about how they'd "take everything," about how nobody understood.

He ignored her.

For all his underground, for all his violence, for all the scary things I'd seen him do in quiet rooms, he still knew there were lines even *he* couldn't cross with cops watching.

He opened the door.

The night spilled in—cool air, flashing red and blue washing over the inside of the house, making everything look even more unreal. The officers stepped in wearing that stiff, practiced calm, eyes scanning the room, taking it all in: the naked woman, the broken glass, the shaking kids on the stairs.

"Ma'am," one of them said, hands held out a little, palms visible. "We're here to help. We need you to put that down."

She laughed.

A hysterical, high-pitched sound that made my skin crawl.

"You're not taking me!" she shrieked. "You're not taking MY CHILDREN!"

Her eyes flared toward the stairs again, locking onto us. I shrank back, but there was nowhere to go. Just the long hallway, the glass door, the bedroom that didn't feel like any kind of refuge anymore.

"She's not right," my father said, voice tight. He sounded more tired than angry now. "She needs help. She's been like this all day—"

"SHUT UP!" she screamed, lunging toward him.

The officers moved at once.

I'd seen my father grab people, move them, hurt them without effort. I'd never seen someone grab *her* like that—two men stepping in, seizing her arms, twisting just enough to keep her from swinging the knife or glass. She thrashed and kicked, wild and uncoordinated, words dissolving into guttural sounds.

For a second, I thought they might hit her.

They didn't.

They talked to her in low, firm voices, using words like *ma'am* and *calm down* and *we're going to get you some help*. She spit at one of them. He wiped his cheek and didn't react, just tightened his grip.

"Kids need to go upstairs," another officer said, looking right at us.

My sister yanked my arm. We stumbled backward down the hallway, away from the stairs, away from the railing, away from the sight of our mother being dragged out of the house screaming.

I caught one last glimpse:

Her head thrown back.

Hair wild.

Mouth open in a sound I couldn't hear over the blood rushing in my ears.

Then the front door slammed.

The sirens started up again outside a minute later.

I stood in the middle of that long, unfinished room, breathing hard, heart punching my ribs. The old boards under my feet seemed to pulse with each beat. The house creaked around me, stretching and settling like nothing had happened.

"She's going to blame you," my sister said finally, voice flat.

I stared at the far wall, at a crack in the plaster that ran from ceiling to floor like a fault line.

"She'll blame *him*," I said, but the words sounded weak even as I said them.

My sister snorted. "She *always* blames you."

There was nothing to say after that.

Later, after the sirens faded and the house went quiet, my father moved through the wreckage downstairs like a man cleaning up after a hurricane. Glass swept into piles. Cushions stacked. Broken frames tossed. Knife or glass wiped and tucked away.

We weren't asked how we were.

We weren't told where she went exactly just that she was "getting help" again. Some hospital. Some place that would hold her for a while and then release her back into our orbit like a storm cloud they'd only borrowed.

When she came home, nothing had really changed.

She didn't remember it the way I did.

In her version, people were against her. They were overreacting. She'd just "had a moment." Everyone made too big a deal out of things.

In my version, she'd torn off the last thin layer
of safety I'd been clinging to.

After that night, the house didn't just *feel*
haunted.
It was.

Not by the Underground Railroad or by the
ghosts of the people who'd hidden in the basement.
Not by creaks or drafts or long hallways at dusk.

By the memory of my mother's naked,
screaming body.
By the sound of my sister's voice, hissing that I
deserved to die.
By the knowledge that even the police couldn't fix
what was wrong with us.

I learned something important that night:
Sometimes the monsters under your bed are the
only place your mind can put the truth,
because admitting they're your own family
is just too much to survive all at once.

I thought that night was the peak.
My mom hauled out screaming.
The cops.
The glass.
My sister hissing that I deserved to die.

I didn't know there was still another scene
coming—
the day they brought my mother back
and took my father away.

CHAPTER TEN

Abandoned

***

They brought my mother home the same day they came for my dad.

I didn't know that's how it was going to work out until I saw the cars.

Police cruisers first parked in front of the Victorian like they'd been there before, which they had. Lights off this time, engines ticking. An unmarked car in the mix. And then another car I didn't recognize, old and dull, idling in the driveway.

My dad took one look out the window and bolted.

He didn't say *run* or *hide* or *don't answer the door*. He just moved. One second he was there, the next he was out the back, cutting across the yard toward the barn like a man who already knew what was coming.

I watched him go, a dark shape against the patchy grass, slipping into the barn door and disappearing.

When I turned back to the front, I saw her.
My mom.
She was sitting in the back seat of the unfamiliar car, like cargo someone had just dropped off. Her hair was flatter, her eyes duller, like the place she'd been—wherever they sent her to "get help"—had

scrubbed some layer of shine off and left her only half-dry.

The driver's door opened. Some worker, some transport person I don't even remember what she looked like now. Just that she walked around and opened the back door for my mother like she was returning a package.

The cops were already heading toward the barn.

It hit me all at once:

They brought her home

and they were taking him away.

Something inside me snapped.

I marched straight out to the car before she could even get both feet on the gravel. The wind cut through my clothes, but I barely felt it. Heat roared in my chest, drowning out everything else.

She looked up at me, eyes glassy, slow to focus.

"Lena, honey " she started.

"You bitch," I spit, the word tearing out of me before I could think about it. "You're taking the only thing I have away from me."

Her face flickered hurt, anger, confusion, all of it swimming together.

"It's not—"

"Yes it is," I snapped. "You told them. You started all this. He's the only thing I had, and now they're taking him because of you."

It didn't matter, in that moment, what he'd done. It didn't matter what his hands had done in the dark or what his rage had looked like up close.

All I could feel was the loss.

The barn door banged in the distance. Voices shouted.

"Come on out, Ray!"
"Don't make this harder!"

Boots on wood.
Someone calling commands.

My mother just stared at me, mouth open like she wanted to argue and couldn't find the words.

Maybe she wanted to tell me she'd tried.
Maybe she wanted to say she loved me.
Maybe she wanted to scream right back.

She didn't do any of that.

She just stood there, half out of the car, watching her husband being dragged out of a barn in handcuffs while her daughter called her a bitch in the driveway.

They walked him past us, wrists pinned behind his back, head high like he could still pretend this was all a joke.

He glanced at me once.

I don't know what I was hoping to see there— an apology, a goodbye, some kind of fatherly anything.

All I saw was a flash of something tired and hard and resigned.

The cruiser door opened.
He ducked his head.
They put him in and shut the door.

Just like that, he was gone.
That's when the file changed.
No longer "Mom unstable, Dad in the house."

Now it was:

Father: incarcerated.

Mother: in the home.

Children: placed with mother.

On paper, this was the part where things were supposed to get better.

After they took my dad, there was this strange, wobbly stretch of time where, on paper, it probably looked like my life should finally be okay.

Dad was in jail.

Mom was home.

My sister was there.

To anyone looking in from the outside, it might have looked like stability.

Inside the Victorian house, it felt like somebody had ripped one entire wall off our lives and left us standing there in the draft, pretending we couldn't feel the wind.

We had rules.

Some were the usual ones do your chores, don't talk back, be home by dark.

And then there was the one about my father:

Never accept collect calls from him.

They said it like he was poison, like his voice alone could crawl through the phone line and infect the house. Answering him wasn't just disobedience; it was betrayal.

"You *do not* take calls from that man," my mother said, eyes narrow, voice sharp enough to cut. "You hear me, Lena? You don't owe him anything."

I did hear her.

I also heard the part she didn't say out loud:

You owe me your loyalty. Pick a side. And it better not be his.

One afternoon, the house was too quiet.

My mother had gone out—some errand, some shopping, something that felt more important to her than being in the same building as me. My sister was somewhere else in the house, tucked into some corner I didn't know, or maybe she'd slipped out, too.

The old rotary phone sat on its little table in the hall, silent and self-important. The kind of phone that rang loud and real, not like the polite chimes in later years.

It went off like an alarm.

RING... RING... RING...

I stared at it for a second, heart picking up speed.

I could've let it go.

Should've let it go.

Instead, I picked up.

"Hello?"

There was a click, a pause, and then the cool, practiced voice of the operator:

"Will you accept a collect call from—"

And then I heard him.

"Lena."

Just my name.

Two syllables, and suddenly I wasn't whatever age I was that day. I was every age at once: three on the camper, six in the flowerbed, eight on the couch with glass in my hair, all the versions of me that had ever turned toward his voice because it meant protection *from* her.

The rule about not accepting collect calls evaporated.

"Yes," I blurted. "Yes, I'll accept."

We didn't talk long. I couldn't tell you the exact words if my life depended on it.

What I remember is the sound of him.
The low rumble of his voice.
The way it wrapped around my name.

There was comfort in it.
There was sorrow in it.
There was something wrong about it, too, now that he was on the other end of a jail line.

But he was still my dad.

For a few precious minutes, it felt like someone saw me again.

Someone cared if I was eating, if I was scared, if the house still creaked too loud at night. I don't know what he promised or what I asked. I just know a part of me unclenched for the first time in weeks.

Then the operator broke back in, and the line went dead.

The spell snapped.

I hung up, the phone heavier in my hand than when I'd picked it up.

By the time my mother came home, my sister had already loaded the gun.

"She talked to him," she said. "She took a collect call."

No warm-up. No hesitation. Just tossed me into the fire.

My mother didn't ask for my side.

She didn't want it.

Her rage came fast—a flash flood. It wasn't a spanking. It wasn't a single smack to scare me straight. It was an *attack*.

Hands, fists, whatever she could get to land. My skin burned.

My ears rang.

I tried not to cry, tried to be the tough girl I'd trained myself to be. But twelve-year-old bodies still cry when they hurt, no matter how much they've been taught that tears are weakness.

"You think you're grown?" she snarled between blows. "You think he cares about you? You think he loves you? You don't *ever* go against me."

By the time she was done, my whole body hummed with pain. My face felt swollen, my arms hot and aching. The edge of my vision had that gray fuzz around it that comes right before you pass out.

"You're not going to the mall with us," she snapped, breathing hard as if *I'd* been the one throwing punches. "You stay here. You don't answer the phone. You don't go anywhere. Do you understand?"

I nodded, because that's what you do when someone is holding your survival in their hands.

She didn't look back as she left.

I watched from the window as my mother and sister got into the car. The engine turned over, the tires rolled, and the Victorian house slowly swallowed the sound of them leaving. Dust rose in a soft cloud behind them on the long driveway.

They got smaller and smaller, and then they were simply gone.

I waited for them to come back.

An hour.

Two.

The way an evening usually goes by when you know someone will walk through the door eventually.

The sun slid down. The house darkened.

I turned on lights as the shadows stretched. The bulbs made the rooms look even emptier corners thrown into harsher relief, the long hallways narrowing into tunnels of yellowed light.

Night fell.

The Victorian house came alive the way old houses do—creaks, pops, distant settling sounds that could be the foundation shifting or could be something else entirely if your imagination ran fast enough.

Given its history, mine did.

I thought of all those people they said had hidden there on the Underground Railroad. How they'd tucked themselves into corners and crawlspaces, listening hard for boots overhead, waiting for help or capture.

Now it was just me.

I checked the cupboards.

Bare.

A few lonely cans, a ripped-open box of something stale. Nothing like enough to feed a girl who'd just been beaten and left behind as punishment.

My stomach gnawed at itself.

I went to bed hungry.

The house exhaled cold around me as I curled on the mattress, every small sound slicing through the dark. Floorboards expanding. Pipes ticking. The wind pushing against old windows just enough to make them whine in their frames.

One night.

Then two.

I rationed what I could find—dry cereal straight from the box, crackers gone soft with age, water from the tap that tasted faintly like rust and dust. Hunger sharpened into something animal, then settled into a dull ache that felt like part of my body.

The sun rose and fell and rose again. I checked the driveway every time I heard an engine, every time tires crunched on distant gravel.

No car pulled in.

No key turned in the lock.

No mother.

No sister.

No one.

I wasn't just scared.

I was *invisible*.

Somewhere out there, my mother and sister were moving through their lives—shopping, eating, sleeping in beds that didn't sit in the middle of a haunted museum of a house.

Somewhere in jail, my father might have pictured me safe at home, trusting that someone was taking care of me.

No one was.

The house pressed in on me, full of other people's ghosts and my living emptiness.

And then, finally, there was a knock at the door.

Not the tentative tap of a neighbor. Not the thunder of police.

A firm, steady knock.

I crept down the hallway, ribs tight, bare feet whispering over the floor. Every instinct screamed at me not to open it too many stories about what could be on the other side.

But the part of me that was starving—physically, emotionally, all of it—turned the knob anyway.

On the porch stood a woman I knew from my father's world.

Elizabeth.

She wasn't family by blood. She wasn't a neighbor. She was one of the people my dad trusted one of the quiet watchers who kept an eye on things when he couldn't.

Her eyes swept over me in one fast, devastating pass.

My thin frame. My hollowed-out expression. The way I hovered in the doorway like a stray animal.

"What are you doing here alone?" she demanded.

Her anger wasn't aimed at me. I could feel that. It vibrated under her skin, but the fury was for the adults, the ones who'd left a child in a ghost-filled house with no food and too many memories.

I opened my mouth.

Nothing came out that made sense.

She didn't wait for an explanation that would only make her more furious.

"Go pack some clothes," she said. "We're leaving."

I moved before I could think, before the house could sink its claws back into me. Threw things into a bag—shirts, jeans, underwear, whatever my hands grabbed first. I didn't know where we were going. I didn't care.

Anywhere was better than being abandoned in the echo of a family that kept choosing to leave me behind.

We walked out together.

Down the long hallway.
Down the stairs.
Out the front door of the Victorian house that looked so impressive from the street and so ugly from the inside.

As we drove away, the house shrank in the rearview mirror. From that distance it finally looked like what everyone else saw—a big, old, beautiful home.

It had all the right bones, all the impressive lines.

And inside, it had just proven what I'd suspected for years:

I could disappear, and the people who were supposed to love me most might not notice for days.

For the first time, though, I was about to find out what it felt like to live in a house where love actually showed up and how fast even that could be taken away.

CHAPTER ELEVEN

Ripped Away Again

***

Elizabeth and her husband lived on a pig farm.

If the Victorian house was all dark hallways and ghosts in the walls, their place felt like a different planet entirely.

The air smelled like hay, mud, and animals—not pleasant, exactly, but *honest*. The kind of smell that said, *This is what we do here*. Not cigarette smoke and burned grease and anger.

Fences crisscrossed the property, sturdy and practical. The barns were old but solid, boards weathered by real work, not fists through drywall.

Inside their house, the noises were softer.

Footsteps.

Chairs pulling out from tables.

Clinking dishes.

No plates shattering against walls.

No screaming that rattled picture frames.

They had a little girl, about seven, with a nickname that made her sound like a candy: **Jelly Bean**.

She had messy hair and bright eyes and the kind of laugh that came out of her whole body. She ran toward me like kids do—no suspicion, no weighing of loyalties—just excited at the idea of a new person to jump on the trampoline with.

For the first time in my life, it felt like I was stepping into an actual family.

Not a perfect one.

Not some TV-movie fantasy.

Just… real.

There were meals at a table where nobody screamed.

Forks clinked. People passed dishes. Voices rose and fell in conversation about normal things—weather, chores, some funny thing the pigs did that day. I didn't have to calculate who was sober enough to stay calm, or who was about to flip the table.

There were rules, but they came with explanations.

"Take your boots off at the door so we don't track mud in," Elizabeth would say, pointing at the mat. "We just cleaned."

Not, "What the hell is wrong with you?" followed by a slap.

Chores were shared, not weaponized.

"Can you help Jelly Bean feed the pigs?" her husband asked once, handing us buckets. His voice wasn't sharp. It was an invitation.

The first time I walked into that barn with her, the pigs nosed at the straw, snorting softly. Dust motes spun in beams of sunlight slicing through gaps in the boards. My boots sank a little into the packed dirt and hay.

"This one's Bacon," Jelly Bean said, pointing. "And that one's Pork Chop."

I laughed, the sound strange in my own mouth.

At night, I lay in a bed that didn't feel haunted.

No sliding glass door to nowhere.

No long hallway full of hidden corners.

Just a small room that smelled faintly of laundry detergent and the sweet, animal-heavy air that drifted in from outside.

I waited for the screaming to start, because that's how nights went in my world.

It didn't.

There were low voices downstairs sometimes, the quiet murmur of grown-ups finishing dishes or talking about the next day's work. A television on low. A sink running.

No one threatened to kill anyone.

No one punched walls.

No one told me I deserved to die.

My shoulders—used to hunching, bracing, flinching—started to loosen, very slowly, like a wild animal uncoiling one muscle at a time.

For a minute, I let myself wonder:

Maybe this is it. Maybe this is where I get to stay. Maybe I finally get to keep something good.

We fell into a rhythm.

School.

Chores.

Dinner.

Trampoline time with Jelly Bean and the neighbor girls.

We'd bounce until our legs burned, hair flying, the sky rolling out above us in a wide, forgiving

blue. The conversations were typical kid stuff—
teachers, crushes we barely understood, giggles
about things we'd overheard older kids say.

One afternoon, we circled a subject that always
comes up eventually when kids are left to stitch
together their understanding of the world:

Sex.

It came out in half-phrases, nervous laughter,
the kind of crude ideas kids pick up from TV and
older siblings and whispered conversations in
school bathrooms. Nothing I said felt particularly
wild. In my head, I was still a kid too, trying to
figure it out like everyone else.

There were things that had already been *done* to
me that those girls couldn't imagine, but I didn't
talk about those.

I didn't have the words.
And even if I did, who would I tell?

Later, Jelly Bean went home.

At some point, her mother asked the question all
parents ask when they hear their kid using words
they're not ready for:

"Where did you learn that?"

"From Lena," Jelly Bean said.

Just three little words.

And with them, the whole story flipped.

It didn't matter that there were other girls on
that trampoline.
It didn't matter that most of what she'd heard came
from a tangle of sources.
It didn't matter that I was still a child myself,

sorting through stolen pieces of information and my own pain.

The blame slid off the faceless group and landed neatly on the easiest target:

Me.

Suddenly, I wasn't the wounded girl from the haunted house anymore.

I was the **bad influence**.
The older girl corrupting the younger one.
The problem.

I saw it in Elizabeth's face when she talked to me. The warmth cooled. The lines around her mouth tightened. Hurt and anger warred in her eyes—not just about what Jelly Bean had said, but about what she *thought* it meant.

"I can't have that here," she said finally.

I don't remember every word. Trauma makes the edges blur. What I do remember is the sensation of the ground shifting under my feet—familiar in a way I had hoped I'd never feel again.

I had done something wrong just by existing in the space where something went wrong.

Again.

"Pack your things," she said.

Those three words were worse than any slap.

I folded clothes into my bag with numb hands, each shirt and pair of jeans going in like proof:

You thought you might be wanted. You were wrong.

The pig farm shrank in the rearview mirror just like the Victorian house had—only this time it hurt more, because I had wanted, desperately, to stay.

For a brief moment, I'd tasted what life could be like when adults remembered to feed you, to ask how your day was, to tuck you in without using your fear as leverage.

I hadn't had it long enough to believe I deserved it.
Just long enough to miss it for the rest of my life.

I didn't know it then, but the next place I landed would be where everything finally shattered, where the person I trusted most would cross a line you can never uncross, and change the girl in the mirror forever.

CHAPTER TWELVE

Morning of Silence

***

By thirteen, I could read that house like a language.

The weight of his boots on the stairs.
The slam of a door that meant *move out of the way*.
The long, stretched quiet that meant *something's coming*.

Most bad days arrived loud.

That morning came in soft.

No screaming. No cupboards banging. Just the low hum of the fridge, a car passing far off on the road, the faint tick of the furnace trying to keep up. The air smelled like old coffee and smoke soaked into the curtains.

I was in my room, half-dressed for school, mind floating somewhere between homework and whether anyone would notice if I wore the same jeans twice that week.

"Lena."

His voice came from down the hall—out of the bedroom he shared with my mother when she was actually there.

"Come here."

He didn't sound mad.

When my dad was angry, his voice rolled, deep and thunderous, like a storm building over water.

This was the smaller version—low, almost casual. It floated down the hallway, not sharp enough to cut.

I went.

Of course I did.

This was still the man who'd pulled my mother off me. The one who stood between me and her worst moods. The one who'd taught me how to hold a wrench, how to look someone in the eye, how to walk into a room like I wasn't prey.

He was danger. He was safety.
Both at the same time.

His room was dim, curtains pulled most of the way closed, morning light slipping in around the edges in thin, dusty beams. He lay on top of the covers, half-propped on pillows, the TV on low with the sound barely a murmur.

He patted the space beside him.

"Lie down," he said.

Every reflex I had was trained from years of being the "good one."

I didn't argue. I didn't ask why.
I just did what I'd always done—I obeyed.

I stretched out on top of the blanket, the same way I had when I was little and cartoons felt safer watched from the crook of his arm than from anywhere else in the house.

For a few seconds, it felt almost normal.

His shoulder beside me. The smell of his soap and smoke and engine oil. The steady rise and fall of his breathing. I stared at the TV, not really seeing it, letting myself sink into that rare moment where nobody was yelling my name.

Then his hand moved.

At first it was just weight. A palm resting on my leg, like he'd done when I was small and fidgety, his touch a quiet reminder to sit still. But the weight slid higher. Slower. Fingers curling, testing.

My whole body went cold and hot at the same time.

He started talking about my mother. How she was gone again. How she didn't want to be there. How he was tired of being alone. Tired of being unwanted.

The words came out low, almost conspiratorial, like we were sharing a secret.

"Someone's gotta take her place," he murmured.

I stared at the TV.

I heard him and didn't hear him, my brain refusing to plug his words into any shape that made sense. Daughters don't "take the place" of wives. That's not a role you fill. That's not… that's not…

His hand slid higher.

Inside, something in me backed away fast, like an animal scrambling into a corner, clawing for any dark place it could disappear.

"Dad…" I whispered.

He shushed me softly, like I was a baby. Like he was calming me down, not tearing something out of me.

"It's okay," he said. "This is just how it is now."

His touch moved into places no father should ever touch. Fingers where they had no right to be. A hot, sick wrongness ran through me, thick as tar.

I didn't have the vocabulary for what was happening.

Words like *molestation*, *abuse*, *incest* lived in after-school specials and health class pamphlets, not in the bed of the man who'd once chased off monsters for me.

What I did have was a body that knew.

My skin crawled. Every nerve screamed *no* while my muscles locked up, frozen solid. Tears pricked at the backs of my eyes, then slipped sideways into my hairline, warm and silent.

I didn't fight.

Girls in movies push and kick and run. I went still.

When you've spent your whole life knowing that fighting back makes things worse, sometimes the only weapon you have left is going limp and leaving your mind.

I focused on the corner of the room, on a crack in the ceiling where the plaster had split into a jagged line. I counted the breaths between the sounds he made. I watched the dust floating in the strip of light by the curtain, tiny pieces of nothing moving in slow spirals.

"You tell anyone, and they'll take you away," he said quietly, breath hot against my ear. "You'll go to some home. You'll never see me again."

It wasn't shouted. It wasn't even a threat in his tone. It was said like a fact.

He'd been my shield against my mother. My rescuer when she'd crossed her own lines. The idea of losing him—of being dropped into some group home with strangers and no one who knew my history—terrified me as much as staying.

He knew that.

He used that.

When it was over, he rolled away like it had been nothing more than a nap. Like he hadn't just taken something from me I didn't know how to name.

"Get ready for school," he said. "You're gonna be late."

I slid off the bed on shaky legs.

The room looked the same.
The bedspread. The TV. The clutter on the dresser.

Only I was different.

In the bathroom, I shut the door and leaned over the sink, gripping the porcelain until my knuckles went white. I turned the faucet on, letting the water roar loud enough to cover the sound of my breathing.

When I finally lifted my face to the mirror, the girl looking back at me had the same brown hair, the same eyes, the same nose I'd always had.

But she wasn't me anymore.

Not just a daughter.
Not just a punching bag for my mother's moods.

Now I was something else:

His child.
His victim.
His secret.

I splashed water on my face, scrubbed harder than necessary, as if I could wash it off—his touch, his breath, the words I never should've heard.

The skin stayed the same color.
The feeling didn't.

I pulled on my clothes with hands that didn't feel completely attached to me, grabbed my bag, and walked out into the hallway.

The house hummed with its usual sounds. The world outside went on like nothing at all had cracked open.

I stepped outside, shut the door behind me, and headed toward the bus stop—

as if the morning hadn't just split my life into a Before and an After.

CHAPTER THIRTEEN

The Secret

***

The strangest part was how normal everything looked.

Same peeling paint on the porch.
Same long driveway.
Same Victorian windows watching the street like always.

The house hadn't changed.

I had.

The world kept expecting the same girl.

I still had to brush my hair.
Still had to answer when teachers called my name.
Still had to remember my locker combination and the homework I'd half-finished the night before.

The world doesn't pause to give shattered girls time to pick up their pieces. It just expects them to keep walking and not bleed on the floor.

At school, the hallways smelled like bleach and old paper. Lockers slammed and squealed. Girls my age compared notes about crushes and school dances, laughing about hand-holding and who might get a kiss under the bleachers.

Every joke that even brushed against sex made my stomach twist.

They were talking about things they wanted someday.

I had just had something forced on me that I'd never asked for.

I walked through the halls feeling like I was made of thin glass. One hard look, one pointed question, and I was sure I'd splinter into a thousand sharp, glittering pieces.

Nobody looked that closely.

Why would they?

On the outside, I was fine. My clothes were clean. I turned my work in. I wasn't failing. I didn't scream in class or cry in the bathroom where anyone could see.

I'd been practicing pretend my whole life.

Now it just had to stretch further.

At home, avoiding him was almost impossible.

This was his territory. His chair. His TV. His kitchen. If I was alone in a room and heard his footsteps coming, my whole body went on high alert. My heart jumped, palms sweating, lungs going shallow.

Sometimes nothing happened.

Sometimes he just walked through, grabbed a coffee, made a comment about the weather, as if his hands had never been anywhere they shouldn't.

On those days, the confusion almost hurt worse.

Which version was real?

The dad who showed me how to change a tire? Or the man who whispered sick things into my hair in the morning?

Both.

That was the hardest part.

Every so often, he'd catch my eye across the room, hold the look a second too long, and say in a low voice meant only for me:

"Remember our little secret. You tell, they'll take you away. You'll never see me again."

He didn't have to raise his voice. The words slid under my skin and stayed there.

I'd already been abandoned in that house once by my mother. Left alone for days like forgotten laundry. I knew what it felt like to be unwanted, to vanish and have no one notice.

The thought of being shipped off to some unknown place, with strangers and strict rules and no one who knew my history, scared me almost as much as him.

So I kept the secret.

I laughed when other people laughed.
Helped set the table.
Did my chores.
Built a shell thick enough to hide what was happening underneath.

Around that time, the house got even more crowded.

Shawn and her husband moved in with their little girl. Then Shirley and her kids came back around. They weren't just random adults drifting through our lives—Shawn and Shirley were my older sisters from my dad and his ex-wife, already grown women with families of their own by the time I was still trying to survive grade school.

The big, nicer bedrooms went to them and their families. It made sense on paper, I guess adults first, families first. The little me could squeeze into whatever space was left.

I got the smallest room.

The floor dipped in the middle where the wood was soft, like one more step would punch my foot straight through to the ceiling below. The walls were close. The window was small. It felt less like a bedroom and more like a storage closet someone had thrown a mattress into.

It should've felt like punishment.

Instead, it felt like distance.

More people in the house meant fewer moments alone with him. More bodies between us. More noise to disguise the way I flinched if he brushed past me in the hallway.

The secret didn't stop.

But the opportunities changed.

Then, suddenly, everything shifted again.

He got a new girlfriend up north. She had three kids of her own and a life that sounded like a twisted version of normal married but separated, a house near a lake, a world that wasn't built entirely out of cigarette smoke and screaming.

"We're moving," he said one day, like he was announcing we were switching brands of cereal.

Part of me sagged with relief.

The Victorian house was soaked in ghosts—of my grandmother's stories, of Underground Railroad whispers, of my mother's naked rage, of bullets through windows and flames on walls.

And now, of that morning.

Maybe somewhere else, those echoes wouldn't follow so loudly.

We packed up our lives in cardboard and plastic.

Boxes stuffed with clothes, tools, pictures nobody ever hung straight. Trash bags full of everything else—old blankets, mismatched shoes, the debris of a life spent surviving rather than organizing.

Rain spat against the windshield as we pulled away from the house for the last time. The sky hung low, gray and heavy, like it was pressing down on the roof as we drove off.

I watched the Victorian shrink in the side mirror.

Big. Beautiful. Terrible.

The cabin up north was smaller, tucked off a quieter road. Trees surrounded it, tall and thick, their tops sighing in the wind. There was a lake nearby, the water a flat sheet of gray-blue that changed mood with the sky.

It was the first time I'd lived anywhere that sounded like nature instead of traffic and fights.

Birds instead of sirens.

Wind in the branches instead of glass breaking. Water lapping at the shore instead of voices hitting walls.

His girlfriend tried to fold me into her life.

There were three kids already bouncing through the house, tracking sand in, arguing over the TV, raiding the fridge like they trusted food would always be there.

She cooked dinners that smelled like actual meals, not whatever could be thrown in a pan fastest. Spaghetti. Meatloaf. Chicken that didn't come burned or half-frozen.

At first, it felt like slipping into someone else's family photo.

I'd walk down to the beach alone sometimes, toes curling in the cool sand, letting the water slide up over my ankles. I'd stand there staring across the surface like I could see a different world on the other side, one where none of the things that had happened in that Victorian house were attached to my name.

School started, and for the first time in my life I went to a regular public high school in a new town where nobody knew my history.

Freshman year.

Fourteen.

Anonymous.

The hallways were wider.

More faces. More noise.

Social rules more layered and confusing than any textbook.

But what I felt most was this:

No one here looked at me and saw "that girl from the big haunted house."

No one saw "the girl whose mother got dragged out by the cops."

No one saw "the girl whose father had turned her into a secret."

They just saw a new kid with a cheap backpack and a fake smile.

In that sea of strangers, I met a boy named Mike.

He was fifteen, all long limbs and easy grins, with that messy hair boys can somehow pull off without trying. He made stupid jokes that actually made me laugh. He looked at my face when I talked, not past me.

We started hanging out at my cousin's place in town.

Her house became my new refuge, a small place with sagging couches and loud music and the constant flow of teenagers in and out. We'd sit on the porch steps, sharing a blanket when it got cold, or pile into the living room and watch movies, arguing about which ones were the best.

For a little while, I almost believed I was just… a normal high school girl.

Walking to and from school.
Nursing a crush.
Pretending what had happened in the Victorian house belonged to some other version of me, some other life.

I thought distance and new walls might be enough to leave it behind.

I didn't understand yet that you can move a girl out of the haunted house,

but you can't move the haunted house out of the
girl—

and that one night, when my dad left me at my
cousin's to go on a date with his new girlfriend,
the past I was trying so hard to outrun was about to
show up in a new body, with a new name, and tear
through what was left of my sense of safety all over
again.

CHAPTER FOURTEEN

Just Another Night at My Cousin's

***

*I*t was supposed to be regular.

Just another night at my cousin's house.
TV on too loud, people drifting in and out, the kind
of teenage Disarray that smelled like cheap
perfume, cigarette smoke, and whatever someone's
m

om had made for dinner hours ago.

My dad dropped me off so he could take his
girlfriend out.

The air outside was cool, sharp enough to make
my breath puff white. The town was quiet in that
small-place way one gas station, one bar, a few cars
humming by on the main road. The sky smeared
with stars you couldn't see back in the bigger cities.

"You good?" he asked from behind the wheel.

I nodded, hand on the door handle.

This arrangement worked for everyone.
He got his night.
I got a place that felt loose and normal.
No Victorian house. No ghosts. No sliding glass
doors to nowhere.

Inside, my cousin's place was warm and bright.

She joked around, moving from room to room,
music playing somewhere in the background.

People came and went, dropping onto couches, heading to the kitchen, curling up in corners with blankets and gossip.

It felt safe enough that my shoulders actually dropped.

I wasn't waiting for a fight to explode.
I wasn't listening for the sound of someone picking up a plate to throw.

I let myself breathe.

Mike came over.

He walked in like he belonged there, easy grin, hands shoved in his pockets. He said hi to everyone, then found me with that particular focus teenage boys get when they've decided you're the person they're there for.

"Hey," he said, softer, just for me.

We ended up in my cousin's bedroom, the door pulled almost shut.

We sat cross-legged on the bed, talking about nothing and everything—teachers we hated, music we liked, stupid stories from school. Our knees brushed. Our shoulders bumped. The conversation looped in circles, the way it does when both people are circling something else.

Then we stopped talking.

We started kissing.

My heart climbed into my throat. It was clumsy and new. His lips were warm, his breath tickling my cheek. My hands didn't quite know where to go, so they hovered, then landed lightly on his shoulders.

This is what girls my age are supposed to do, I told myself.

Have crushes.

Kiss boys.

Learn what it feels like to be wanted in a way that isn't about violence.

For a moment, it almost worked.

Then he reached over and turned off the light.

The room changed.

In the dark, the familiar outlines of my cousin's posters and furniture dissolved. The air felt heavier. The bed seemed smaller. My brain did that thing it did whenever the lights went out in dangerous places:

Went backward.

Back to my father's room.

Back to that low voice.

Back to hands that didn't stop when I said no.

My chest tightened.

My skin crawled.

Mike's hands started to move—down my sides, over my stomach, pushing past the edge of what I was okay with.

"Stop," I whispered. "No."

The word slipped out before I could swallow it back. It hung there between us in the dark, fragile and small.

He didn't pause.

His hands kept going, more insistent now, exploring places I didn't want touched.

My heartbeat slammed against my ribs.

"Mike," I said, louder. "No. I don't want to."

He hushed me. Told me it was fine. Told me this was normal. His weight shifted, pressing me down. The mattress dipped under us, springs complaining.

My mind split.

Part of me was still there squinting into the dark, feeling his breath on my neck, hearing my own voice say *no*.

The other part left.

Floated up toward the ceiling, toward the corner where shadows pooled. Watched the scene like it was happening to some other girl. Some other body. Some other life.

I had learned how to do that in my father's bed. Now I was using it to survive in my cousin's.

He didn't stop.

The room got quieter even as my thoughts screamed. My body stiffened, then went limp, the way bodies do when they realize resistance is just another way to get hurt.

Time blurred.

When it was finally over, the darkness felt heavier than before.

The air smelled like sweat and something sour that clung to the back of my throat. My clothes were twisted. My skin burned in places it hadn't before.

I sat there in the dark and thought:

It happened again.

Different house.

Different bed.

Different boy.

Same feeling.

I didn't have the right words lined up in my brain.

Assault.

Rape.

Those were vocabulary words in health class. Plot points in TV movies. Things that happened to other girls who had dramatic music swelling underneath their stories.

In my head, it landed like confirmation of something I'd been half-believing for years:

No matter where I went, no matter what roof I slept under,

my body was never really mine.

When Mike finally left the room, I straightened my clothes in the dark, moved my hair back from my face with shaky fingers, and walked out like nothing had happened.

No one stopped me in the hallway.

No one looked too closely.

No one said, "Are you okay?"

By the time my dad's truck pulled up outside later, my mask was back on.

"How was it?" he asked, as I climbed in.

"Fine," I said.

I didn't tell him.

Who would he have been in that story—

the protector I needed,

or a reflection of the man who'd already taught me that "no" didn't matter?

We drove back to the cabin.

I went back to school.

Days lined up like always—classrooms, lake water, small talk, chores.

On the outside, nothing had changed.

Inside, another piece of me had gone dark and quiet.

I thought, *Nothing can surprise me anymore.*

I was wrong.

CHAPTER FIFTEEN

The Raid

***

*T*rouble never really left my dad alone. It trailed him like a shadow he couldn't outrun.

It was only a matter of time before it found us up north.

One night when I was about fifteen, he went out to the Moose Lodge—one of those small-town places where men drank cheap beer under fluorescent lights and pretended they weren't running from themselves.

His girlfriend went too.
So did her ex-husband.

That combination alone was a bad idea waiting to happen.

Out in the parking lot, the night air was cold and thin. Words got sharp. Old resentments bubbled up. Lines that used to be blurred suddenly looked like battlefields.

Shoves.
Yelling.
All the usual pre-fight choreography.

Then the ex pulled a knife.

For most people, that would be the climax of the story.
Big scary moment. Cops called. Everyone goes home and tells the tale.

But my father wasn't most people.

He'd been trained in a war that lived
underground, in tunnels, in hand-to-hand decisions
about who walked out and who didn't. He'd earned
a reputation in quieter rooms long before that night.

Backing down wasn't in his wiring.

He got the knife away from the man.

And then he used it.

By the time the news reached me, I was staying
over at Mike's place, trying to play at normal
teenage life.

We were hanging out with his family, TV on,
some casserole smell drifting from the kitchen,
everything too ordinary for the words that dropped
into the room:

"Your dad stabbed somebody."

The world did that tilt again.
Like a film reel slipping off track for a second.

Stabbed.
Not shoved.
Not punched.

Stabbed.

Details came in messy pieces, parking lot,
Moose Lodge, girlfriend's ex, blood, sirens. Adults
whispered in the next room, their voices low and
urgent, while I sat there on the couch, feeling like I
was underwater.

I didn't know if the man was alive or dead.
I didn't know where my father was.
I just knew the ground under my life had cracked
even deeper.

We went to the cabin to grab some of my things.

It was dark by the time we pulled up. The trees stood tall and black against the sky, branches shifting in the wind. The place looked normal from the outside—no lights flashing, no cars lined up in the drive.

Inside, it felt wrong.

Too quiet.

Too still.

Like the house itself was holding its breath.

"Just grab what you need and we'll go," someone said behind me, Mike, or his mom, or both. My ears buzzed too loud to pin the voices down.

I stepped inside.

The cabin smelled like it always did—pine cleaner, cigarettes, the faint dampness that came from being so close to the lake. My stuff was where I'd left it. Clothes in a pile. School books on the little table. A hairbrush on the counter.

My dad wasn't there.

I moved through the rooms fast, tossing things into a bag. Jeans. Shirts. Underwear. A couple of small things that made the place feel like mine a cheap bracelet, a photo.

I was zipping the bag when everything exploded.

Shouts outside.

Boots pounding on the steps.

A crash as the door flew open so hard it banged against the wall.

"POLICE! DON'T MOVE!"

The room filled with men and uniforms and guns, all at once, like they'd materialized out of the dark.

Red dots landed on my chest.

For a second, I didn't even understand what I was seeing just little circles of light fluttering on my body, on the furniture, on the walls.

Then my brain caught up:

Laser sights.

On guns.

Pointed at me.

My hands shot up without my permission, fingers spread wide.

My heart was beating so hard I could feel it in my throat, in my ears, in the backs of my eyes. The bag slipped from my shoulder and hit the floor with a dull thud.

"Don't move," one of them repeated.

I stood there in my own living room, if you could call it mine, with my hands in the air, like every cop show I'd ever seen, except there were no cameras, no commercial breaks, no guarantee that they understood I was just a kid.

I hadn't held the knife.

I hadn't thrown a punch.

I hadn't made a single choice that led to that parking lot.

It didn't matter.

In their eyes, I wasn't Paige or Lena or anybody with a story. I was just another piece of the scene.

Part of the mess that came attached to my father's name.

Questions came fast.

"Where is he?"
"When did you see him last?"
"Who else lives here?"

My mouth answered on autopilot, words coming out small and shaky. My eyes stayed locked on the barrel of the closest gun, on the tiny circle of darkness at its center.

I wondered, bizarrely, if this was how it ended not with my father's violence finally catching up to him, but with someone else's mistake ricocheting into my body.

They searched the cabin, tearing through what little we owned. Drawers yanked out. Cushions tossed aside. Cabinets flung open. The whole place flipped upside down in minutes.

My life had already been a series of upheavals. Now strangers were rearranging even that.

Eventually, someone realized I was just a teenage girl with a bag of clothes and nowhere else to go.

The guns lowered.
The shouting softened.
But the damage was already done.

I never really put my hands down after that—not inside myself.

Even when my arms dropped to my sides, some other part of me stayed frozen in that living room, red dots on my chest, waiting to see what would happen next.

They didn't arrest me.

They didn't read me rights.

They did something that, in their minds, probably felt like rescue.

They called CPS.

I didn't walk out of that cabin with a suitcase and a plan.

I was taken
out of my father's house,
out of the only world I knew,

And then I was thrown into a new kind of hell I never saw coming foster care.

CHAPTER SIXTEEN

Intake

***

*T*hey didn't call it being taken.

They called it **placement**.
Like I was an object that needed a better shelf.

After the raid at the cabin, my life got boiled down to paperwork and acronyms.

CPS.
DHS.
Foster care.

A woman showed up in a blazer that didn't quite fit and a face that was trying to be kind without getting too attached. She had a clipboard, a folder with my name on it, and a voice she kept soft, like she was talking to a skittish animal.

"We just want to make sure you're safe," she said.

I'd heard versions of that line my whole life. From cops. From counselors. From teachers.

Safe meant different things to different people.

To her, it meant "not with your father, who just stabbed someone in a parking lot."
To me, it meant "somewhere nobody hits me or touches me or leaves me alone for days."

We weren't using the same dictionary.

They took me in a state car—one of those four-door sedans with nothing personal inside. No crumbs in the floorboards. No toys. No CDs. Just a

stack of files on the front seat and the faint smell of
stale coffee.

I sat in the back, hands in my lap, staring out at
trees and road signs blurring past.

Nobody asked if I wanted the radio on.
Nobody asked if I was hungry.

The social worker tried small talk.

"What grade are you in?"
"Do you like school?"
"Any brothers or sisters?"

I answered in short bursts, words clipped.

"Ninth."
"It's okay."
"Yes."

I didn't tell her the real answers.

That school was the only place I'd ever felt
close to normal.
That I'd already lived a dozen lives before most
kids my age had even stayed up past midnight.
That I had siblings scattered through the mess of my
parents' relationships like forgotten toys—some by
blood, some by choice, some who wished I didn't
exist.

"We've got a good home lined up for you," she
said, like it mattered. "Nice family. Stable. They've
been fostering for a long time."

Good. Nice. Stable.

Words that sounded like TV commercials.

We pulled up to a squat brick building first—
intake. Because before you could get placed on a
shelf, they had to label the box.

Inside, the air was too cold. The fluorescent
lights hummed. Plastic chairs lined the walls,
molded in the shape of people who'd been forced to
sit and wait for things they didn't ask for.

They took my bag and went through it.

Held up my shirts.
Shook out my jeans.
Checked pockets like I might be smuggling
weapons or secrets in the seams.

I stood there while they catalogued my life:
Two pairs of jeans.
Four T-shirts.
A couple of bras and underwear.
One bent photo.
A cheap bracelet.
A notebook with doodles on the cover.

It didn't look like much when they laid it all out.
It didn't look like a whole childhood.
Just looked like stuff.

They handed me a paper cup of water and
pointed to a bathroom.

"In there," someone said. "We need to do a
quick physical check. Make sure you're okay."

Those words again.
Make sure you're okay.

They had forms to fill out marks to note, bruises
to record, anything that might scream "lawsuit"
later if they didn't write it down.

"Take off your shirt," the nurse said.

She wasn't cruel. She wasn't gentle, either. Just
tired. Efficient.

I peeled my T-shirt off, arms stiff, the cold air hitting my skin like a slap. Under the harsh lights, every scar, every faded bruise, every mark had nowhere to hide.

She made notes on a clipboard.

"Those from a fall?" she asked, pointing to an older bruise on my shoulder.

"Yeah," I lied.

Maybe it had been.

Maybe it hadn't.

After a certain point, all the impacts blurred together.

She checked my arms, my back, my legs. Asked if anyone had ever hurt me "in a sexual way."

I paused for half a second too long.

Her eyes flicked up.

"Has anyone ever touched you where they weren't supposed to?" she rephrased, like maybe the wording was the problem.

I thought of my dad.

Of his breath hot against my ear.

Of the way he'd said, *This is just how it is now.*

I thought of Mike.

Of the dark room.

Of my own voice saying *no* that didn't matter.

"Yes," I said, but so quietly it barely counted.

Her pen hovered.

"Who?"

"My dad," I whispered. "And… some boy."

I didn't say their names. Saying them out loud felt like dragging them into the room with us.

She wrote something down.
Box checked.
Question answered.

No one hugged me.

No one said, *I'm so sorry that happened to you.*

Just: "Thank you for telling me," in a voice that was already moving on to the next line of the form.

Back in the lobby, the social worker smiled like she thought maybe the edges of this could still be smoothed.

"Ready to go meet your foster family?" she asked.

Ready?

I hadn't been ready for anything in my life.
Not the camper.
Not the horse.
Not the grease fire.
Not the knife.
Not the cops.
Not my father's hands.

But I nodded.
Because what else was there to do?

We got back in the car.

The sun was sliding down, the sky streaked orange and pink. It would have been pretty, if I'd had space in my chest for things like that.

We drove through a subdivision this time.

Houses that all looked like variations of the same idea—two stories, small porches, trimmed lawns, bikes tipped over in driveways. No bullet holes in the siding. No police tape.

Kids played in a yard as we passed—kicking a ball, shrieking with laughter.

They looked like a different species.

"Here we are," the social worker said, pulling into a driveway halfway down the block.

The house in front of us had blue shutters and a wreath on the door. Flowers in pots. A porch light that glowed warm, not harsh.

It looked like the kind of place where people baked cookies for holidays and took pictures on the steps.

My stomach flipped.

Good home. Nice family. Stable.

We were about to find out what those words actually meant.

CHAPTER SEVENTEEN

The House of Rules

***

The foster mom met us at the door with a smile that didn't quite reach her eyes.

The house behind her wasn't some neat little subdivision special. It was an old farmhouse tired siding, sagging porch boards, the kind of place that looked like it had seen too many winters and not enough repairs.

"You must be Lena," she said, voice bright and careful.

I nodded.

She smelled like fabric softener and something faintly floral. Her hair was set the way older women wore it, soft curls sprayed into place. She was in her sixties, at least. Her blouse and slacks looked ironed within an inch of their life. Everything about her was neat. Controlled.

Not a wrinkle out of place.

Inside, the house opened into a big living room that tried to look cozy but felt… off. There were two staircases—one on each end of the room like someone had decided the best way to slice up kids was by side of the house.

Each staircase led up to two bedrooms. One of the rooms was big enough to cram two girls in. The others were smaller, boxes with beds lined up against the walls.

Off the living room, there were two more doors. One was the foster parents' room. The other was reserved for the oldest foster girl, like a prize you earned if you lasted long enough.

Down below everything, in the basement, a massive wood stove did the real work of keeping the place alive in winter. The heat drifted up unevenly, so some rooms baked while others stayed cold and damp.

"There are five other girls here right now," the foster mom said, like she was giving a tour of a boarding school instead of a state-run holding pen. "We run a very structured home."

Structured.

Another word people liked to use instead of the truth:

Control.

The social worker trailed behind us, file tucked under her arm like a safety blanket. We all gathered around the scarred kitchen table me, the foster mom, the social worker, and the foster dad, who wandered in from somewhere in back, wiping his hands on a rag that looked as old as the house.

He was quieter. Watchful. The kind of man who took in a room without saying much. His eyes slid over me, then away, but they lingered a half-second too long.

They talked over my head at first.

Her: "What's the case plan?"

Social worker: "Dad is in jail pending trial. Mother

is… not a safe option at this time."

Him: "Any known behaviors?"

Behaviors.

Like I was a dog that might chew the furniture.

The social worker flipped through my file.

"Significant trauma history," she said, like it was one item on a grocery list. "Some suspected sexual abuse."

My face burned.

They all glanced at me, then quickly away, like I was a car accident they didn't want to look at too long.

"We can handle that," the foster mom said.

She didn't say it unkindly.

She said it like a challenge.

The social worker slid some papers across the table.

"These are the house rules," the foster mom said, tapping them with her manicured finger. "Curfew, chores, expectations. We believe in structure, respect, and consequences."

I looked at the list.

No TV after 8 p.m. on school nights.

No phone calls past nine.

Chores assigned weekly.

Must ask permission before leaving the house for any reason.

Church every Sunday.

Youth group on Wednesdays.

It didn't sound so bad on paper.

I'd grown up with rules too.

They just came with fists and knives and threats, not laminated sheets on the fridge.

After the social worker left, the house changed.

The foster mom's polite smile dropped about three degrees.

"Your room is upstairs," she said. "You'll be sharing with the other girls. We keep things tidy here. No food upstairs. No closed doors unless you're changing. Do you understand?"

I nodded again.

Agree.

Adapt.

Disappear into whatever shape made their lives easier.

She led me up the staircase on the left.

The bedroom she pointed me into had two beds, two dressers, and barely enough space between them to turn around. Clothes were folded into piles. Shoes lined up under the beds. Another girl glanced up at me, then quickly went back to what she was doing, like she'd learned not to get too attached to anyone new.

"You can put your things away," the foster mom said. "Dinner's at six. We don't call kids twice."

She left me with my trash bag of clothes and my too-small life.

I unpacked slowly.

Each folded shirt into the drawer felt like proof I wasn't going home.

Not to the Victorian house, not to the cabin, not to anywhere that had my father's fingerprints on it.

A clock ticked somewhere down the hall.

The whole place smelled like wood smoke, something baking, and too many lives layered over each other.

At dinner, we all sat around the same scarred table.

Foster mom at one end.

Foster dad at the other.

Five girls packed between them in mismatched chairs.

Plates were set at every spot. Food passed in bowls—potatoes, meat, vegetables that hadn't come from a can for once.

"Lena, would you say grace?" the foster mom asked.

My fork froze halfway to my mouth.

I hadn't been to church regularly since before the knife at the door. My conversation with God, if you could call it that, was mostly me asking why he hated me so much.

"I… don't really…" I started.

She smiled, but there was steel behind it.

"Well, you're welcome to pass," she said, "but in this house, we bow our heads and show respect. Bill, you do it."

The foster dad bowed his head. The girls followed. I stared at my plate for a second, then dropped my gaze too, more out of not wanting to stand out than out of faith.

"Lord, thank you for this food, for this home, and for bringing Lena to us," he said.

Brought.

Like God had personally signed the placement papers and not some overworked caseworker with a stack of files on her desk.

"Amen," everyone said.

We ate.

The food was good. Real. My body didn't care about my pride; it devoured everything in front of me like it was afraid this was a one-time thing.

The foster mom watched.

Not in a creepy way.

In a measuring way.

Later, the girls scattered. Some went upstairs. One curled up in the living room with a book. Another disappeared into the "oldest girl" bedroom off the living room like it was a throne room.

Chores came next.

Dishes.

Sweeping.

Bringing up an armload of wood from the basement to feed the hungry stove that heated all of us whether we liked it or not.

Nights were the worst.

From my bed, I could hear the old house breathing—wood popping, pipes clanking, the low hum of that stove below us. I also heard other things.

Footsteps on the stairs when everyone was supposed to be asleep.

The front door opening.

Whispers.

Giggling that didn't sound happy.

More than once, I watched from the shadows at the top of the stairs as the foster dad quietly led one of the older girls out the front door late at night.

They'd come back smelling like cigarettes and cheap alcohol, stumbling a little, faces flushed in a way that didn't have anything to do with church or chores.

It twisted my stomach.

I'd seen enough by then to know what "special treatment" usually cost a girl.

One afternoon, I tried to do what I thought you were supposed to do.

I caught the foster mom alone in the kitchen, sorting mail at the table.

"I don't think he should be taking girls out like that at night," I said, my voice shaking. "They come back drunk. It's not right."

Her hands froze for half a second.

Then she set the letters down, folded her fingers together, and looked at me with an expression that could've cut glass.

"Young lady," she said quietly, "in this house, we do not spread lies. We do not cause trouble. We are grateful for what we've been given. Do you understand me?"

"I'm not lying," I whispered. "I've seen—"

"That's enough," she snapped.

By dinner, my punishment was already in place.

"No phone calls," she announced. "No letters in or out for Lena until she can learn some respect and stop making up stories."

It didn't matter that I didn't really get any phone calls or letters anyway.

It wasn't about cutting me off from anyone.

It was about sending a message:

We decide what is true in this house.

We decide what gets seen.

We decide what gets said.

Later, in my borrowed bed, I stared at the cracked ceiling and made mental lists.

Pros:

- No screaming.
- Nobody drunk and raging.
- Food.
- Bed with no springs poking through.

Cons:

- Rules that shifted when you bumped them.
- Eyes on me all the time.
- Secrets no one wanted to admit existed.
- No space to be messy, or angry, or anything other than grateful.

I wanted to be grateful.

I knew what the alternative looked like gun sights and jail calls and cops at the door. I knew that in a lineup of bad options, this house would probably rank near the top.

But that didn't undo the years before it.

It didn't erase my father's hands.
It didn't unteach my body that I was an object
people used and blamed.

In the darkness, I whispered into my pillow:

"Don't cause trouble. Don't get sent away. Just
last. Just make it."

It became my new rule, layered on top of theirs.

I didn't know yet that no matter how quiet I
stayed, no matter how hard I tried to be the "good
foster kid," the cracks would still show.
and that this old farmhouse, with its wood stove and
Bible verses and smiling photos, would become the
place that smiled for church on Sundays while
quietly stripping girls of more than just their
clothes.

CHAPTER EIGHTEEN

Price Tag

***

*I*t took me a while to realize I came with a price tag.

At first, the foster house just felt like a different kind of strict.

There were chore charts taped to the side of the old fridge, scribbled names and days held up by weak magnets. The vacuum had a place. The mop had a place. The wood for the stove was stacked just so in the basement.

I didn't. Not really.

I was slotted into their life like an extra item on the list:

- Trash out on Tuesdays
- Bathrooms on Saturday
- Lena

I tried to follow every rule.

Up by six.

Bed made.

Hair brushed.

"Yes, ma'am," "No, sir."

I'd survived houses where breaking rules meant knives and cops and holes in the wall. I figured I could handle a place where breaking them meant lectures and lost TV time.

But underneath the Bible verses on the walls
and the chore charts on the fridge, something mean
lived in that house.

I caught little pieces of it in whispers.

"State pays pretty decent for teenagers."
"At least we get something back for the trouble."
"Her mom's an engineer at GM. You know she's
paying support."

I'd be wiping the counters, or folding towels, or
walking past the kitchen when the talking dropped
low and my name slipped into the air with other
words:

"spoiled"
"ungrateful"
"thinks she's better than everyone"

I didn't even own that much.

A couple pairs of jeans.
A few nice shirts my dad had bought back when the
Agent Orange money came in and he was trying to
buy the future he knew he couldn't give any other
way.

That settlement had been meant for me.

For what the war did to him.
For what the chemicals might do to me someday.
For some kind of chance beyond dirt floors and raid
nights.

His ex-girlfriend got to it first.

She took that money and turned it into new
siding and shiny cupboards, fresh paint and new
flooring. My "future" became someone else's open-

concept kitchen. Every board nailed down was another dollar I'd never see.

By the time I hit that foster house, whatever was left of that dream was numbers on someone else's paperwork.

That Christmas, one of my sisters sent me a card.

The foster mom handed it over without looking inside, the way she always did with stuff from "trusted family." Just my name on the envelope in a familiar hand, a little slanted from hurrying at a kitchen table somewhere that wasn't mine.

I opened it at the table.

The card itself was simple some winter scene and a pre-printed message but tucked inside was eight crisp hundred-dollar bills. Eight hundred dollars. More money than I'd ever held in my life with my own name on it.

Before I could even process it, her hand shot out.

"We'll take that," she said, plucking the money out of the card like it had always belonged to her. "This will go toward Christmas for the girls. That's what being a family is all about everybody shares."

Shares.

They spent it on presents for the foster girls. Clothes. Little things. Wrapping paper and bows.

Nothing was bought just for me.

My name had been on the envelope. My sister had sent it to me. But watching those bills disappear into their budget drove the point home harder than any lecture:

Even when money had my name on it, it still didn't really belong to me.

On top of that, my mom was paying seven hundred and fifty dollars a week in child support to that foster family. Seven hundred and fifty dollars every week, just to keep me in that old farmhouse with the wood stove and the chore charts.

"The state pays us for her," the foster mom said once, not knowing I was in earshot. "And her mother sends support. There is no reason she should act like we owe her anything."

I stood frozen in the hallway, heart pounding.

I hadn't asked them for anything.

I ate what they gave me.

Wore what I had.

Kept my head down.

But in their minds, my existence was a spreadsheet.

Income in one column.

Inconvenience in the other.

They looked at my clothes and decided it meant I'd "had everything handed" to me.

"You don't know what real struggle is," the foster mom said one day when I hesitated to hand over a jacket my dad had bought me. "Those kids in the other rooms? They've never had anything nice. You can share."

Share.

That sounded reasonable. Kind, even.

But "share" turned into "give."

They started passing my clothes down to the other girls and kids who dropped in and out of the house. Shirts I loved. Jeans that finally fit right. The jacket that made me feel like I looked like other girls at school instead of the girl from the haunted Victorian.

"Oh, they fit her better," the foster mom would say. "You'll grow out of it."

I was still wearing them just fine.

Watching my things disappear piece by piece felt familiar in a way that made my teeth ache.

My childhood had been a long lesson in how quickly you could be moved, shoved, thrown, taken. Now even my clothes weren't really mine.

You are not yours.
You are ours to move, to punish, to judge, to strip down.

That was the message, over and over.

The boys in the house got away with things I never could.

They forgot chores and got reminded.
I forgot and got a lecture about being "lucky to be here."

They snapped at her and she said, "Teenagers, right?"
I answered with the wrong tone and heard, "You can always go back to where you came from."

As if I had a map back.
As if there was a "back" that wasn't burning.

Sometimes we'd all be in the living room—TV on, plates on our laps, some family movie playing—and I'd catch her studying me.

Not watching the show.
Watching me.

Her eyes would slide over my face like she was weighing something.

"Don't look so miserable," she'd say. "You've got it better than you ever did before."

She wasn't entirely wrong.

No one was throwing plates.
No one was pulling knives.
No one was touching me in the dark.

But safety isn't just the absence of obvious danger.

Sometimes it's the presence of being wanted.

I didn't feel wanted.

I felt managed.

A caseworker came by once a month.

She'd sit at the table with her folder, asking questions in that same careful tone.

"How are things going here?"
"Are you getting along with everyone?"
"Do you feel safe?"

I'd shrug and say, "Yeah, it's fine," because what was I supposed to say?

Well, I'm not getting punched, so that's an upgrade. But I'm also being treated like a walking check with an attitude problem.

She'd nod, jot something down, and close the file.

"Good. Keep up the good work."

Like I was earning a grade in surviving.

Underneath all of it, something started to build.

A pressure in my chest, in my throat, in the back of my skull. All the things I'd swallowed for years—the horse and the camper and the fire and the night at the Moose Lodge, my father's hands and Mike's breath in a dark room—stirred.

The foster mom's lectures scratched at that pile like a match.

"Your father is a criminal."

"Your mother is a mess."

"You're lucky we even took you."

Lucky.

Like being plucked out of one fire and put in a smaller, tidier one was a prize.

One night, I lay in bed staring at the floral pattern on the ceiling, rage and grief braided together so tight I couldn't tell them apart anymore.

They thought they knew my story.
They thought I was some spoiled brat who needed structure.

They had no idea what I'd already survived to sit at their table and say "yes ma'am" with my hands folded.

The next time the caseworker came and asked, "Is there anything you want to talk about?"

the word "no" rose to my mouth—

and something else finally shoved past it.

"Yes," I said.

My voice shook.
My hands did too.
But I started talking.
About my dad.
About the Victorian house.
About the cabin and the knives and the raids.
About what he'd done in the mornings when the
house was quiet.
The caseworker's eyes widened. Her pen, for
once, stopped moving.
The words felt like broken glass coming out.
Sharp.
Painful.
Impossible to swallow again once they'd started.
I thought telling would help.
That saying it out loud would finally pull me out
of the shadows.
I didn't know yet that in this world,
a girl like me telling the truth could be treated like
the worst crime of all—
and that the system meant to protect me would
find a way to punish me for opening my mouth.

CHAPTER NINETEEN

Arizona

***

When I finally opened my mouth in Michigan and started hinting at what my life had really been like, the system's answer wasn't therapy or a hug.

It was a plane ticket.

"Family placement," they called it. "Kinship care."

Like those words alone were enough to guarantee safety.

They started looking at options. My mother wasn't one. My father sure as hell wasn't. So they turned to the next layer out—the older daughters he'd had before me.

They chose **Shawn**.

One of his older girls. Living all the way in Arizona.

On paper, she looked good.

Steady job. Stable address. Husband. Kids.

She told them she was willing to take me.

They stamped that as *fit placement* like it was that simple:

Teenage girl with a history of violence, abandonment, and sexual abuse

- Half-sister in another state
  = Problem solved.

Nobody asked if she really knew what she was signing up for.

They didn't ask if she knew what had happened in the Victorian house, or the cabin, or how many times I'd already been uprooted and replanted like some half-dead bush.

They booked my flight.

The airport smelled like recycled breath, burnt coffee, perfume that clung too hard to strangers' coats. I held a one-way ticket in my hand and watched Michigan fall away through a scratched plane window—green turning to patchwork, patchwork turning to shapeless color.

Maybe this will be it, I thought.
Maybe this will finally be a home that lasts.

Arizona hit me like another planet.

The air was dry instead of heavy.
The sun felt sharper, like it had teeth.
The colors were wrong—browns and reds and pale yellows instead of damp greens and gray skies.

Shawn's house sat in a neat row of other neat houses—stucco, desert landscaping, gravel instead of grass. Inside, it was all clean lines and normal furniture.

Couch not ripped.
Walls not punched.
Pictures straight, not hiding holes.

It looked like the kind of place people mean when they say "family home."

At first, she tried.

There were rules, but they came with explanations.

"Be home by nine so I know you're safe." "Help with dishes, everyone does their part." "Homework before TV."

Her husband sat with me sometimes at the table, pencil in hand, walking me through math problems that had knotted in my brain.

"No, look," he'd say, patient. "You move the x over here. Try this way."

He didn't talk to me like I was stupid. He talked to me like I could learn.

I soaked it up like a plant that had gone too long without water.

To me, he was just a grown-up doing what grown-ups were supposed to do:

Help.

Guide.

Show up.

To Shawn, it was something else.

"You only help her because she's here," she snapped at him one day, voice sharp as snapped glass. "You never did that for me."

He blinked, caught off guard.

"I'm… helping both of you," he said, but the words landed flat.

It didn't matter that we were different ages, different people, in different chapters of life. In her

head, I'd been dropped into a competition I didn't
even know I was in.

Her jealousy wrapped around me like a fence.

She watched how he talked to me.

How I answered.

What I said about my past.

Every story I told turned into a test.

At first, I talked the way I always had: in pieces,
sideways, hinting.

About the Victorian house.

About Michigan winters and snowmobiles.

About fires and bullets and the way my parents tore
each other apart.

"Sometimes," I said quietly one night, "it felt
like they didn't really want me."

Shawn frowned.

"That didn't happen," she said. "You're lying.
You have such an imagination."

There it was again.

That word.

Imagination.

I'd heard it from Michigan foster parents, from
teachers who thought I was being dramatic, from
caseworkers who only read the bullet points in my
file.

Imagination was easier to swallow than reality.

Because if they believed me, then they had to
accept that parents really did throw kids off
campers, aim horses at them, threaten them with
knives, leave them alone in haunted houses, and

crawl into bed with them like they weren't their own children.

Imagination was safer.

For them.

Not for me.

The more she dismissed my past, the more something twisted inside me.

If every adult in every new house agreed I was exaggerating, maybe I was.

Maybe I *was* dramatic.

Maybe the horse, the fire, the beatings, the cabin—maybe I'd turned them into something bigger than they were.

The problem with gaslighting a kid who's survived real horror is that they've already been taught not to trust themselves.

You don't have to push very hard to make them fall.

Eventually, I started to push back the only ways I knew how.

If I was going to be treated like the bad one, I might as well act like it.

I started drinking with the neighbor—cheap alcohol passed back and forth over fences and on porches, burning my throat but numbing the ache.

At school, I met a boy who lived down the road.

We'd skip class together sometimes, drifting through the neighborhood instead of sitting in desks. The desert sun beat down on us as we walked, the heat pressing through my black T-shirt like a warning and a dare.

On paper, it looked like I was "acting out."

In reality, I was just trying to breathe in a life where my choices still belonged to caseworkers and court dates.

At home, every move I made became another mark against me.

"You're using too much phone time."
"Why didn't you fold the towels the right way?"
"Why are you looking at me like that?"

Her eyes tracked me constantly, a ledger ticking up in the back of her mind.

Every story I told about Michigan, every time I laughed at her husband's jokes, every time I came in five minutes later than she wanted—
all of it went in the "problem" column.

It didn't matter that I was still going to school.
That I wasn't stealing.
That I wasn't hitting anyone.

I was a foster kid in her house.
The bar was higher.
And it moved every time I got close to reaching it.

I tried to stay out of the way.

Spent more time at the neighbor's.
Stayed longer at school.
Took the long route home, dragging my feet in the dust.

But the house always waited.
So did her watching.

I didn't know it yet, but it didn't matter what I did or didn't do.

She'd already decided what story she wanted to tell about me—
and one night, she picked up the phone and made it official.

CHAPTER TWENTY

Runaway on Paper

***

$\mathcal{T}$he night everything broke in Arizona, I wasn't

outside.

I wasn't sneaking off.

I wasn't hiding.

I was standing in Shawn's house.

Right there.

In the living room.

Within arm's reach.

We'd been tense all day.

Her eyes on me like I was mold she'd found in her fridge—proof something in the house was spoiling, and she'd traced the smell back to me.

I don't remember what tiny thing lit the fuse.

A look.

A word.

A slammed cupboard door.

In families like ours, the trigger never really matters. The explosion is already waiting. It just needs an excuse.

At some point, something inside her clicked.

She walked over to the phone.

Picked it up.

Dialed.

Her gaze locked on mine the whole time, like she wanted me to watch what she was about to do.

"Shawn, what are you doing?" I asked, my throat already tight.

She didn't answer me.

Instead, she spoke into the receiver in a calm, clear voice.

"I need to report a runaway," she said. "My foster kid. She ran away."

My stomach dropped so fast it felt like the floor fell out beneath me.

"I'm right here," I said, voice cracking. Tears stung the backs of my eyes. "I'm literally right here."

She turned slightly away, putting her shoulder between me and the phone like I might reach over and snatch the words back from the air.

"Yes," she continued. "She left. I don't know where she is."

Her words carried more weight than my entire existence.

Because she was the homeowner.
The foster parent.
The adult with the matching last name on the mailbox and the paperwork in order.

I was the teenage girl with a file thick enough to choke on.

Her version of events had power before I even opened my mouth.

I could've screamed.
Thrashed.
Begged.

But I already knew how this worked.

Grown woman's word
versus
fifteen-year-old "troubled foster kid" in black eyeliner and too much history.

Guess who the world believes?

The cops didn't rush in with guns drawn this time.

They came with measured steps and practiced faces, hands resting near their belts, eyes scanning the room like they were already filling in the report in their heads.

"Where is she?" one of them asked Shawn.

She pointed at me.

"There," she said. "But she ran away earlier. She's out of control. I can't handle her anymore."

Out of control.

Those words landed like a verdict.

"I didn't run away," I said. "I've been here. I was standing *right here* when she called."

The officer glanced between us.

Shawn: hair neat, clothes clean, house in order.
Me: foster kid with a record of skipping school, drinking, "attitude."

Her story didn't have to be good.
It just had to be simple.

"Pack a bag," the cop said to me, voice more
tired than cruel. "You need to come with us."
I wanted to scream *why?*
Why is her lie worth more than my truth?
Why does everyone keep saying they want me to be
honest and then punish me when I am?
Instead, I did what I'd done my whole life.
I obeyed.
Hands trembling, I went to my room.
Stuffed clothes into a bag.
Left behind the pieces of a life I'd just started to
believe might be mine.
When I walked back out, Shawn wouldn't meet
my eyes.
The cops didn't cuff me.
They didn't drag me.
They just escorted me out of the house like a
package being returned—
mis-sent, mislabeled, not their problem anymore.
The desert air was cold on my skin.
I slid into the back of the cruiser, the door
shutting with a solid, final *chunk* behind me. The
neighborhood lights blurred past through the
window.
I pressed my forehead to the glass and watched
the house shrink.
It had never really been mine.
But losing it still hurt.

They took me to a group home.

Concrete floors.

White walls that had seen everything and said nothing.

Institutional furniture bolted to the ground like they were afraid even the chairs might run.

There were other girls there.

Each with their own files, their own collapses, their own versions of "out of control." We slept in rows of beds, our lives lined up like mismatched shoes—similar shapes, different scuff marks.

Staff came and went.

Some were kind in small ways—extra mashed potatoes at dinner, a smuggled magazine, a soft voice when nightmares woke us up.

Some were hard, voices clipped, eyes narrowed, already jaded by too many girls like us coming and going.

At intake, they wrote my name on paperwork, assigned me a bed, handed me a sheet of rules.

Again.

Lights out at ten.

No leaving the property without permission.

No closed doors.

Chores posted on a chart.

My entire life had become variations of the same list.

Once again, I was a file number first.

A human second.

The group home wasn't meant to be forever. Just a holding pen while the adults decided what to do with me next.

Keep her in Arizona?
Send her somewhere else in-state?
Ship her back to Michigan like damaged mail
returned to sender?

Eventually, they chose the last option.

"Your case is being transferred back," a staff
member said flatly one afternoon, as if that sentence
didn't rip another root out of the ground. "You'll be
going back to Michigan."

Back to where it had started.
Back to the state that had taken me from the cabin
and placed me with people who'd called me spoiled
and dramatic.
Back to the place holding my memories like stains I
couldn't wash out.

They didn't send me back as the same girl,
though.

Arizona had taught me something new:
You can be in the house, following the rules, not
running at all—

and someone can still dial the phone, look right
at you,
and call you a runaway.

They can write a story about you while you're
standing in the room and watch as the world
believes them.

CHAPTER TWENTY-ONE

Telling

***

*T*he home I came back to in Michigan was only temporary.

It was a quiet, neat little Christian home. The foster dad was a pastor, the kind of man who prayed before meals without making a show of it and spoke to me like I was a person, not a project. The foster mom was kind in a soft, tired way—extra potatoes on my plate, an extra blanket folded at the end of the bed without a big speech about it.

There were rules, but they didn't crack like whips.

"Call if you're going to be late."
"Let us know where you are."
"Try your best in school."

For a minute, I let myself breathe.

I started to think, *Maybe this is what it could have been like all along.*

Then, about a month later, the call came.

The old farmhouse foster home—the one with the wood stove in the basement and Bible verses on the walls and a price tag on my head—had decided they wanted me back.

They "demanded" it, is how it was explained to me.

They told the system I'd been *their* foster kid, that they still had a bed for me, that they were willing to "take me on again." No one said out loud that they'd also lost my support checks when I left.

So, paperwork shuffled.

The nice Christian home became a layover instead of a landing.

And I was shipped back.

Back to Michigan, they slotted me into another foster home.

only this time it wasn't new.

Different month.

Same address.

Same parents.

Same setup.

Chores.

Curfews.

School.

Rules taped to refrigerators.

I'd lost count of how many roofs I'd slept under by then. Each one came with its own version of "we're here to help" that always sounded just a little rehearsed.

By that point, I was done trying to impress anybody.

I went to school.

Did my work.

Came home.

Followed the basic rules.

And I started talking.

Not all at once.

Not everything.

Just enough to test the air.

With counselors.
With social workers.
With whoever's job it was that day to ask me how I
was doing.

"My childhood was… rough," I'd say.

They'd nod in that professional way.

"What do you mean by rough?"
"Can you give me an example?"

I'd watch their faces as I dropped pieces of my
life on the table like puzzle bits.

"My dad wasn't always… safe."
"There was a lot of violence."
"I've seen him stab someone."
"I've had guns pointed in my direction."

Sometimes they'd tilt their heads, faces soft
with practiced pity.

"You've had a rough childhood," they'd say.
"But maybe you see it more dramatically than it
was."

"Maybe you have a big imagination."
Imagination.
Again.

That word was like a trigger now. It made me
want to flip tables, scream, claw my own skin off.

I didn't imagine hooves pounding the ground as
a horse came straight at me.
I didn't imagine glass raining down on my head
when a bullet tore through our window.
I didn't imagine my father's voice in the dark telling
me I'd never see him again if I told.

Still, their doubt wormed in.

If every adult kept suggesting maybe I'd made it worse in my head, maybe I had.

Maybe I was crazy.

Eventually, one counselor asked a question I can't even remember now.

Something about going home.

Or how I felt about my dad.

Or what I was afraid of.

Whatever it was, it hit a fault line inside me that had been waiting to crack.

"I need to tell you something," I said.

She looked at me differently then.

More alert.

Like she heard the fracture in my voice even before the words.

I told her.

Not everything, not yet. My throat wouldn't let the full story out in one go. But enough.

The morning in his bed.

His hand moving where it had no right to be.

The words *this is just how it is now*.

The threats about foster homes and never seeing him again.

The words came out jagged.

My chest burned.

My hands shook.

I watched her face like it might decide whether I lived or died.

I braced for it:

You're exaggerating.
You're dramatic.
You're making things up.

She didn't say any of that.

Her eyes hardened—but not at me.
Her jaw set—not into rejection, but into anger
pointed outward.

"I believe you," she said.

Three words I'd never heard from an adult about
my trauma. Not like that. Not straight. Not without
a "but" attached.

Believe.

The floor shifted.

She brought in a specialist.

Someone whose job wasn't just to listen, but to
investigate.

He met me in a small office with beige walls
and a table that had seen too many confessions.

He didn't talk down to me.
He didn't rush.
He didn't look at the clock.

He asked me to start at the beginning.

So I did.

I told him about the first time in my father's
bed.
About the way the house was quiet.
About cartoons humming in the background like
nothing was wrong.

I told him how it happened again later, at the ex-
girlfriend's house, at the cabin. How the pattern felt
like a loop I kept getting trapped in.

He didn't look away.

He didn't roll his eyes or sigh like I was repeating myself.

He took notes.

Asked careful questions.

Clarified without blaming.

When I finally ran out of words, my throat felt like sandpaper. There's a special kind of exhaustion that comes from dragging secrets out of your body. It feels like you've run a marathon without moving.

"Thank you for telling me," he said. "This is serious. We're going to look into it."

He meant it.

There were exams.

More interviews.

People asking me to go over it again and again, tugging on details I'd tried to bury.

For the first time, the system's weight leaned even slightly in my direction.

My father was charged.

There would be a trial.

A courtroom.

A judge.

A jury.

A chance for me to stand up and say, in public, what he'd done with him sitting right there.

Everyone around me called it justice.

"This is good," they said. "You'll finally be heard. He'll finally be held accountable."

It was supposed to feel like victory.

It felt like standing at the edge of a cliff with everyone behind me chanting *jump*.

Because telling in a counselor's office is one thing.

Telling in a courtroom full of strangers, with your abuser watching your mouth every time it opens—
that's another monster.

Still, some part of me clung to the hope:

Tell the truth.
They believe you.
He gets punished.
You get to move on.

Nobody told me that sometimes the truth breaks you open in public, then quietly leaves you to bleed on your own.

CHAPTER TWENTY-TWO

The Courtroom

***

Courtrooms on TV look big.

High ceilings, polished wood, lawyers pacing dramatically. The music swells, the camera zooms in, and the whole world seems to tilt toward justice.

Real court is smaller.

The air smells like old paper and sweat. The fluorescent lights buzz. The benches creak when people shift their weight. There's no soundtrack, just coughs, shuffling feet, and the occasional throat being cleared like someone's trying to swallow words they don't want to say out loud.

Before I ever stepped into that room, there was another scene no one in the jury box would ever see.

My mom came to visit me at the foster home.

It was the first time she'd come to see me there.

I remember straightening my bedspread, picking up the few things I owned, like somehow if my little foster room looked neat enough, she might want to take me out of it.

I watched from the window as a car pulled up.

When she walked in, she looked smaller than I remembered and sharper at the same time—like someone had taken sandpaper to her edges.

For a minute, I was just a kid again, hoping.

We sat in the generic living room that belonged to every foster home—neutral couch, mismatched throw pillows, a coffee table with some old magazines. A worker hovered nearby, giving us "privacy" that still had eyes.

I finally asked the question that had been chewing through me for months.

"Why don't you just take me out of here?" I said. "Why can't I come home?"

She stared at me for a long time.

When she finally spoke, her voice was flat in a way that hurt worse than yelling.

"I can't stand to look at you," she said. "You're his rape child."

The words hit like a slap.

Not *my daughter.*

Not *my baby.*

Not *what he did was wrong.*

Just: *his rape child.*

Like he owned even that part of me.

Something in my chest folded up on itself.

I didn't know where to put my hands. My face burned. The room felt too bright and too small at the same time.

The worker shifted, like she'd heard it but didn't know what to do with it either.

There was no big blowup after that. No dramatic exit.

The visit ended.

She left.

I stayed.

When the day of court came, that sentence came
with me.

You're his rape child.

It sat under my skin like a live wire as they got
me ready, as they drove me to the courthouse, as
they told me I was brave and doing the right thing.

The first time I walked into the courtroom, my
legs felt like they belonged to someone else.

I'd dressed as "good" as I could.

Plain shirt.

Jeans without holes.

Hair pulled back.

I wanted to look like the kind of girl people
believed.

Not dramatic.

Not wild.

Not the "troubled foster kid" written in thick ink all
over my file.

He was already there.

My father sat at the defense table in a button-
down shirt that didn't fit quite right, sleeves a little
too long. His hair was combed, his beard trimmed.
From a distance, he could have been any working
man at a meeting he didn't want to attend.

He turned when I came in.

Our eyes met.

For a second, the courtroom disappeared.

It was just him and me again,
the man who'd taught me to ride, to wrench, to walk
with my head up even when I was terrified,
and the same man who'd pulled me into his bed and

rewired my understanding of what the word *father* could hold.

His face did something complicated.

A flicker of guilt.

A flash of anger.

Something like hurt, like he couldn't believe I was actually going through with this.

I looked away first.

I couldn't stand the weight of his stare. It felt like standing under a sky full of storm clouds waiting to open.

They swore me in.

"Do you swear to tell the truth, the whole truth, and nothing but the truth?"

My hand was raised. My palm felt sweaty against the air.

"I do," I said.

I'd been telling versions of this story for months to counselors, caseworkers, investigators, doctors.

This was different.

Every word was being recorded.

Every pause could be picked apart.

Every detail could be used for or against me.

The prosecutor's questions came first.

He was careful.

Gentle, in an official sort of way.

"How old were you when this happened?"

"Where were you living at the time?"

"Can you tell the court what your father did?"

I answered in pieces.

My voice shook, but it didn't break at first.
Once I started, the story dragged itself out of me
like it had been waiting at the back of my throat,
banging on my ribs to be let out.

The bed.
The cartoon sounds.
His hand moving where it should never have been.
The words he'd whispered: *This is just how it is
now.*

I didn't use pretty phrases.
I didn't use legal terms.
I just said it the way it had happened, as straight as I
could.

Then they asked me to point at him.
"Can you indicate for the court where the person
is who you say did these things?"

He was right there.
He'd always been right there in my memory.

I lifted my hand, halfway.
My finger shook.
And then my eyes met his again.
Everything I'd ever seen him do flashed through
me at once—
the knives, the fights, the guns, the way he'd stared
down cops, the way people were afraid of him, the
way *I* had been afraid of him my whole life.

All the threats.
All the warnings.
*You tell, they'll take you away. You'll never see me
again.*

Suddenly it wasn't just a courtroom anymore. It was every room he'd ever filled with danger.

My throat closed.

The walls tilted.

"I can't do this," I heard myself say.

At first it came out small.

"I… I can't do this."

Then louder, breaking apart.

"I CAN'T DO THIS!"

It tore out of me, over and over, like my body was trying to claw its way off the stand.

The judge said my name.

The prosecutor said my name.

Somewhere, my caseworker's voice tried to cut through the roaring in my ears.

My face was wet.

I hadn't even realized I was crying until I couldn't see the jury anymore.

"I can't," I sobbed. "I can't. I can't."

The judge called a recess.

Everything blurred.

Someone took my elbow.

Someone led me out of the courtroom.

The door shut behind me with a heavy thud.

Out in the hallway, my legs gave out and I slid down the wall, sucking in air that felt too thin.

"You did your best," somebody said.

"It's okay," somebody else said.

It didn't feel okay.

It felt like I had just broken something important and I didn't even know how to name it.

Inside that room, the case kept going without
me.

Lawyers argued.
Motions were filed.
Words like *credibility* and *reasonable doubt* floated
over my head in conversations I wasn't invited to.

All I knew was that I had finally made it into the
one place where everyone said the truth mattered
most—

and when I looked the truth in the face,
wearing my father's features,
my fear was louder than my voice.

I didn't know yet how the jury would see that:
not as a terrified child facing her abuser,
but as a story that suddenly didn't look clean
enough to convict.

CHAPTER TWENTY-THREE

The Verdict

***

They didn't make me sit in the courtroom for
the verdict.

"Do you want to be there?" someone asked—
my caseworker, maybe, or the counselor who'd
tried to help me practice for testifying.

I thought about it.

About going back into that room where my
voice had collapsed.
About sitting there while twelve strangers decided
what they believed about a story I hadn't been able
to get all the way out.

"No," I said.

Some part of me already knew that whatever
they said, it wasn't going to fix anything inside me.

I waited somewhere else,
another office, another hallway, another borrowed
chair in another building that wasn't really mine.

When the call came, the words were simple.

"He was found not guilty."

Not.

Guilty.

Three syllables that hit harder than a punch.

The label not guilty didn't mean he hadn't done
it.

It meant the story, the fear, the broken little girl
on the stand, the meltdown—
none of it added up to enough in their eyes.

Reasonable doubt.

That's what they called it.

To me, it felt like they'd held my life up to the
light and decided it was too smudged to be believed.

Somewhere, he walked out of that courtroom
free.

My father—
Ray, the racer, the man in the trophy room,
the one who'd once lifted me out of crushed
flowerbeds and bragged about my fearlessness—
walked away.

I sat on the edge of a bed in yet another foster
room and stared at the floor, feeling like I was the
one who'd been sentenced.

What came next felt like betrayal layered on
betrayal.

The same system that had told me *We believe
you*
started using a different word for what I'd said:

Perjury.

They said my statements didn't match.
What I'd told counselors.
What I'd told investigators.
What I managed to get out on the stand before fear
swallowed me.

They said I had lied under oath.

I hadn't lied.

I had choked.

I had stood in front of the man I was most afraid of in the world and felt every threat he'd ever made wrap around my throat.

I was a kid who had watched him stab people, aim guns, rage at cops, disappear into barns and basements when things got hot.

I knew what he was capable of.

If he walked free
and decided I'd ruined his life,
what else might he do?

No one wanted to hear that part.

They wanted clean lines.

True or false.
Yes or no.

The law didn't have a checkbox for *I was terrified for my life*.

So they charged me.

Perjury.

I was still a minor.
Still in foster care.
Still bouncing between roofs and caseworkers.

And now I was also "the girl who lied in court."

I remember pieces, not the whole thing.

A meeting in an office that smelled like coffee and toner, someone explaining the charge in words too big for the age I actually was inside.

"You said one thing before and something different later."
"If they can't trust your testimony, it's perjury."
"There are consequences for that."

An overworked lawyer I barely knew telling me what was "best."

Standing in front of another judge while grown-ups talked around me.

My name echoing through a room that didn't feel like mine anymore.

Perjury.

They said it so casually, like they were talking about a parking ticket.

Inside, it felt like being told:

Not only did we not protect you—
we're going to punish you for not being brave enough, steady enough, perfect enough in the way you told us how we failed.

Later, the state did something that almost didn't feel real.

A worker sat me down and said they were going to change my name.

Not just a nickname.
Not just a "you can call yourself this if you want."

My full legal name.

"Your dad knows how to find you," they said. "This will make it harder. It's for your protection."

Paperwork moved.
Forms were filled out.
Signatures scribbled by people who barely knew me.

On one set of documents, the girl I had been up to that point stopped existing.

On another set, a new name appeared—
a version of me the state hoped he couldn't track.
It was supposed to be safety.
In some ways, it was.
But it also felt like erasure.
Like the girl he'd hurt
and the girl who tried to tell
both got buried under a fresh label and a file
number.
Family faded.
Shirley, Shawn, the others—my older sisters
from his first marriage, the ones who had known the
angry man, the violent father, the underground
figure people whispered about—
chose him.
Word filtered back to me in bits and pieces.
"She lied."
"She made it up."
"She tried to put him in prison."
Not *He hurt her.*
Not *He took advantage of his own daughter.*
Just: *She ruined his life.*
I became the villain in their story.
Not the child whose body had been stolen,
but the girl who had dared to step into a courtroom
and then fallen apart.

The state considered my case "resolved" once
all the paperwork was done.
Case closed.
No conviction.

Perjury on the kid.
Name changed.

On some screen, somewhere, I probably became a few lines of text:

Minor witness.
Allegation.
Defendant acquitted.
Perjury adjudication.
Name change for safety.

Resolved.

As if my story ended there.

It didn't.

All that non-guilty verdict did was carve another line through my life:

Before I told

and

after I learned what it cost.

Before, I'd been the girl nobody wanted to claim.

After, I was still that girl—
only now I was also the one the system had labeled untrustworthy

for being too scared to stand steady in front of the man who had taught me fear.

I thought, *Maybe someday I'll find a way to tell this whole thing without breaking.*

I didn't know yet how long it would take to unlearn the lessons carved into me:

That love always comes with a knife.
That safety is temporary.

That telling the truth might save you,
and still cost you everything at the same time.
    But even underneath the shame,
underneath the new name and the old fear,
    there was a small, stubborn ember:
    A belief that my story was still mine—
and that one day, I'd write it down exactly how it
happened
    so no one could ever again say
it was just my imagination.

CHAPTER TWENTY-FOUR

A New Name

***

The court case was over.

The adults stamped it: **resolved**.

My father was in prison.
The state had a verdict it could file away.

But systems don't just let girls like me walk away and "get on with life."
They always seem to have one more form, one more idea, one more way to rearrange you.

This time, it was **protective custody** and a **new name**.

"The people he ran with… they might not be happy," someone explained in a small office. A worker I barely knew, with a folder that had my life inside it and my new "status" on the tab. "If they blame you, they could come looking."

They said it like I wasn't already looking over my shoulder everywhere I went.

The solution, on paper, sounded simple and reasonable and almost kind:
Change her name.
Seal her records.
Make it hard for anyone to find her.

Like I was a witness being tucked into a new life by some federal program, not a girl who'd already been moved more times than most people move furniture.

"New name, clean slate," the worker said. "This is a good thing."

In their mouths, *good* and *safe* got used like duct tape—slapped over anything they didn't know how to fix.

In my chest, it felt like something else:

Erasure.

Again.

I didn't get a big courtroom moment for it. No dramatic reading of my old name, no speeches. A judge signed papers in a room I wasn't in. Clerks stamped things. Numbers changed in boxes on forms.

One day, someone drove me to a dull government building with beige walls and flickering lights.

"You'll sign here," they said, putting a stack of papers in front of me. "This makes it official."

I stared at the lines.

The old name—the one tangled up with my father, my mother, the camper, the horse, the Victorian house, every house after—was printed at the top.

Underneath: a new one.

A stranger's name.

A name that had never been yelled down a hallway. Never been written on a school incident report. Never been signed at the bottom of a police statement.

"Do I have to?" I asked.

"It's for your own good," they said.

Those words had followed me my whole life.

For your own good, stay quiet.

For your own good, don't answer his calls.

For your own good, don't tell anyone what happens in this house.

For your own good, move here / move there / try again / start over.

I signed.

The pen felt heavy in my hand.

My hand shook just enough that the letters wobbled.

Walked into the building as one version of me.

Walked out as someone else—

at least as far as the law was concerned.

Same bones.

Same scars.

Same nightmares.

Different name.

They called it protection.

It felt like proof that I didn't belong to anyone.

Not my father.

Not my mother.

Not even to the name I'd survived under.

The state had taken my father away.

Now it took my old self, too, and filed her in a cabinet under a label that said **do not open**.

On paper, I was safer.

In my body, I was just… less.

Less visible.

Less real.

Less *mine*.

The only thing that didn't change was the one
fact no system can re-label:
I was still the girl who had to figure out what to
do with all of it—
under whatever name they gave me.

*The state could change the letters people used to
call me,
but it couldn't give me what I wanted most:
a family who showed up and stayed—
especially on the one day that was supposed to be
all about me.*

CHAPTER TWENTY-FIVE

The Open House

***

Senior year is supposed to be a victory lap.

You're meant to glide through the halls knowing you survived freshman awkwardness, bad haircuts, and all the tiny social wars no one remembers later. You're supposed to talk about prom and college and "the future" like it's a thing you can actually see.

With my new name and yet another foster home, I got something close to… normal.

This family wasn't perfect.
No one slammed doors off hinges.
No one threw plates.

There were rules, but they weren't weapons.

"Call if you're going to be late."
"Let us know who you're with."
"Do your homework, do your chores, don't be an ass."

Reasonable.

They had kids of their own. They squeezed me into the mix like an extra puzzle piece that didn't quite match the picture, but they tried.

There were dinners at a table.
Homework spread out on counters.
School events they actually showed up for.

For a little while, I got to pretend that maybe this was what it felt like to belong.

Not "you're our project."
Not "you're our paycheck."
Just: "You live here. Grab a plate."

I got a boyfriend.
A job.
A routine.

We talked about graduation like it was actually going to happen. A real diploma with my new name printed in official ink.

"Of course we'll throw you an open house," my foster mom said. "Every senior gets one."

I tried to play it cool.

"Yeah, sure," I said. "If you want."

Inside, my heart leaned toward the idea like a plant to sunlight.

An open house.

Tables with food.
A sheet cake with my name on it.
Pictures on a poster board that said, "Look, she made it."

The day came.

They decorated the yard.
Hung streamers.
Set out plastic tablecloths that flapped in the breeze.

A long folding table held bowls of chips, trays of sandwiches, a cake with frosting that wasn't fancy but still had my name written across it in looping letters.

They'd done the work.
Done the thing people do for their own kids.

I stood there in my cap and gown, hands smoothing the fabric over and over, watching the driveway.

Cars slowed.

Some rolled by without stopping.

A few turned in, hesitated, and pulled back out like they'd gotten the wrong address.

Neighbors had been told.

Family had been told.

People who "knew me" had been invited.

The house stayed quiet.

The food sweated under plastic wrap.

The streamers fluttered.

The clock ticked.

I laughed too loud at nothing, shrugged too hard.

"It's fine," I said to my foster mom. "People are busy. I didn't expect much."

Inside, every minute that passed sank a little deeper into me.

I had changed my name.

Stood in court.

Moved houses like other kids changed shoes.

I'd survived parents who should have destroyed me.

Surely I was worth an afternoon.

One car finally pulled in and parked.

My boyfriend climbed out.

So did his parents.

They carried a card and a small gift bag, the tissue paper puffed up like it had something important to protect. They hugged me like they meant it, like this was the only party that mattered today.

"We wouldn't miss it," his mom said, smiling.

We ate cake.

We talked.

We took a few pictures.

If anyone drove by and glanced over, it probably looked like a quiet little party, small but normal.

I knew the truth:

This was supposed to be the moment all my "moves" and "services" and "interventions" led up to. The state's unspoken promise: endure the process, and you'll step into adulthood with a circle around you.

Instead, my circle was exactly three people who didn't share my blood and owed me nothing.

When they left, the yard felt even emptier.

We stacked the leftover plates.

Wrapped the uneaten food.

My foster parents said the right things.

"People are flaky."

"Schedules are crazy."

"It's not about you."

But the driveway had already answered for them.

On the outside, I shrugged it off.

"I'm not really a party person anyway," I joked.

On the inside, it carved itself into stone:

Even with a new name,

even with a clean legal slate,

I was still the girl no one claimed
even on the one day meant to celebrate that I'd
made it out alive.

If I wanted any kind of future,
I was going to have to build it myself
even if that meant starting adulthood alone,
sleeping in a car in a field instead of the home I kept
hoping would appear.
They didn't say it cruelly, but a few days after
graduation my foster mom sat me at the kitchen
table and folded her hands like she was about to
pray. Instead, she explained how "the checks stop
now," how I was technically an adult, how they'd
"done their part." I could stay for "a little bit," she
said, but I needed to be out by the end of the month.
No plan. No apartment lined up. No savings that
could stretch that far. Just a deadline and a garbage
bag of clothes.
That was how I stepped into adulthood: not with
a launch, but with a notice.
Congratulations, you made it.
Now get out.

CHAPTER TWENTY-SIX

Car in the Field

***

𝓘 was barely out of high school when I learned what adulthood looked like for a girl like me. My first place of my own wasn't a cute apartment with mismatched furniture and plants in the window.

It was a car.

A 1983 Ford Escort hatchback.

Brown, with big rust holes eating through the exterior on the driver's side door.

Faded paint.

Smelled like nursing home scrubs and long shifts.

Seats permanently indented from lives before mine.

I had a full-time job.

Evenings and nights as a CENA in a nursing home.

Clocked in.

Clocked out.

Turned residents. Fed them. Changed them.

Calmed them down at three in the morning when they were confused and scared.

I could keep other people's parents and grandparents comfortable.

What I couldn't do was afford rent.

Before I got the Escort, there were nights I handed half my paycheck to a taxi driver just to get to work and back. I'd ride in the back seat in my scrubs, watching the meter climb and thinking how every mile was money I wasn't saving for anything else.

Now I finally had a car—
just not a home.
So when my shift ended, my coworkers went home
to roommates and rent and arguments about dishes
in sinks.
I drove to a field.
It was just far enough outside of town to be mostly
forgotten, but close enough that I could drag myself
back into the world half-awake in the mornings.
Grass grew tall around the edges.
The ground was rutted from trucks and seasons.
I'd pull in, park facing away from the road, kill the
engine, and listen to the ticks and pops of the metal
cooling.
This was my "bedroom."
I learned how to fold myself into the driver's seat,
knees up, blanket over my legs. Window cracked
just enough to let air in without letting too much of
the night in with it.
The radio became my nightlight.
The dashboard glow became my lamp.
Every sound outside made my body tense.
A branch scratching the side of the car.
Distant tires on gravel.
Wind pushing against the frame hard enough to
rock it.
I wasn't afraid of ghosts anymore.
I was afraid of being found.
Found by cops.
Found by someone who'd decide they had rights to
my body because they'd found me alone.

Found by anyone who might see a girl sleeping in a car and smell weakness.

Some nights, fear didn't wait for a sound outside. It came from inside my own head. I'd jolt awake in the middle of that dark, silent field, heart pounding, sure I was back in that mean foster home—the one that rifled through my things and gave my clothes away to other girls like I was a donation pile instead of a person. For a few seconds I could feel that house around me again, hear their voices calling me spoiled for wanting to keep the only nice things I owned.

Then the reality would seep back in: steering wheel under my fingers, cold glass against my cheek, the rusted door to my left instead of a bedroom I didn't belong in. I'd lie there reminding myself:

You're not there.

You're in your car.

They can't take anything from you here.

In the mornings, I'd drive to a gas station bathroom.

Brush my teeth in a stained sink.

Splash water on my face.

Hide my bag under the hand dryer while I fixed my hair.

By the time I pulled into work, I looked… fine.

Tired, maybe.

But fine.

Nobody knew that my "commute" was from the middle of a field.

"That's what you get for leaving," a voice in my
head whispered sometimes—my mother's tone, my
father's logic, a chorus of foster rules.
You didn't stay.
You didn't behave perfectly.
You didn't make yourself easy enough to keep.
This is what alone looks like.
But under that shame, another feeling lived:
Stubbornness.
No one could throw me out of this car.
No one could box my clothes and decide where I
went next.
No one could call the cops and label me a runaway
while I stood in the room.
It was pathetic.
It was terrifying.
It was also the first time in my life that the roof over
my head—metal and dented as it was—was under
my control.
I promised myself:
This is temporary.
One day, there will be four walls.
One day, there will be a door that locks from the
inside, and no one else will have the key.
:

When that day finally came,
I thought having my own apartment would mean the
ghosts would calm down,
but all a quiet place really did was make their
voices easier to hear.

CHAPTER TWENTY-SEVEN

Four Walls

***

*M*y first apartment wasn't much to look at.

Peeling paint.
Thin carpet that had seen better decades.
Kitchen cabinets that stuck if you didn't yank them just right.

To me, it might as well have been a castle.

I'd saved enough for a deposit and first month's rent, hustled my way through the application without a co-signer, and convinced a landlord I wouldn't be trouble.

"I work full-time," I told him. "You'll get your money."

He glanced at my new name, at the lack of rental history, at the way I stood too straight, like I was holding myself together with muscle and willpower.

"Don't have parties," he said. "Don't piss off the neighbors. Pay on time."

Deal.

When I turned the key that first day and walked in, the emptiness rang.

No furniture yet.
Just bare floors and echoing walls.
My footsteps sounded like someone else's.

I dropped my bag in the middle of the living room and just… stood there.

No one yelling from another room.
No one's moods to gauge before crossing the space.
No one listening to see if I'd answer the phone
when I wasn't "supposed" to.

Just a cheap apartment and a girl who'd never
had a place that was truly hers.

I slept on a blanket on the floor at first.

Sometimes ate cereal out of a mixing bowl
because I didn't own real dishes yet. Used a box as
a nightstand, another as a table.

It didn't matter.

The lock on the door turned from the *inside*.

If someone came pounding in the middle of the
night, it would be for the wrong apartment, not
because my parents had done something again.

The building had its own sounds.

Neighbors arguing through thin walls.
Baby crying two floors down.
Pipes knocking when someone turned the water on.
Distant traffic humming like white noise.

This was what safety sounded like to me:

Not silence—that always meant danger in my
childhood.
Not perfection, that was never real.

Just the steady, ordinary noise of other people
living their own lives, not mine.

Of course, the ghosts came with me.

Not the Victorian kind.
The memory kind.

The horse.
The camper.

The bullet through the window.
The fire.
The Victorian house.
The pig farm.
Arizona.
The group home.
The courtroom.
The car in the field.

They all sat with me on that floor some nights while I stared at the blank wall and wondered what it would take to feel… clean.

Safe.
Worthy.
Real.

Four walls didn't heal the damage.
But they did give me someplace solid to start from.

In that little apartment, with its second-hand lamp and sloping floor, I finally had something no system could stamp, move, or rename:

A place where I could sit with my story and start untangling it.

Piece by piece.
Chapter by chapter.

Until someday, it wouldn't just live in my head. It would live on a page,

in my own words, under my own name, so no one could ever again call it "just my imagination."

CHAPTER TWENTY-EIGHT

Haunted

***

On paper, I finally looked stable: a job, a
cheap apartment, my own key on my own ring.
People think the past lives in old houses.

In my case, it moved in with me.

It didn't matter that the Victorian was miles
away, that the cabin was someone else's problem
now, that the pig farm, the group home, Arizona, the
field—were all behind me.

The ghosts didn't need an address.

Even in that first cheap apartment, they knew
exactly where I slept.

They didn't slam doors or rattle chains.
They came quieter.

In the middle of the night, when the building
had settled and even the neighbors' TVs had gone
dark, my own brain turned on me.

I'd wake up with my heart going a hundred
miles an hour, sheets twisted around my legs like
I'd been fighting something in my sleep. Sweat
cooled on my skin. My eyes would lock on the
shadows in the corners.

For a few seconds, I wasn't in my apartment.

I was back in the Victorian hallway, staring at a
glass door that opened to nothing.
Back on the couch with glass in my hair.
Back in my father's bed with his hand moving

where it never should have been.

Back in Arizona, watching a woman call me a runaway while I stood three feet away.

My body didn't know where "here" was.

It just knew *danger*.

Sometimes, I'd bolt upright and claw at my throat, convinced I could feel the slice of a knife that had never actually landed. My dad's words would echo in the dark:

If you run, I'll catch you. I'll slice your throats.

There were nights I slept with the light on, the overhead bulb buzzing like a fly, because darkness felt too much like memory. Other nights, I'd turn off every light and sit with my back against the wall, staring at the front door to make sure it stayed closed.

"Why are you so jumpy?" coworkers would ask when I flinched at a slammed drawer or a raised voice.

I didn't know how to explain that to someone who'd grown up in one house and slept through the night.

How do you tell someone:

When you've been trained since childhood to listen for danger, silence doesn't feel calm. It feels like the two seconds before impact.

My nervous system never got the memo that we'd moved.

I still scanned every room for exits.

Still sat where I could see the door.

Still tensed when a man walked behind me.

Even the good ones.

Especially the good ones.

A hand on my shoulder could feel like a threat and a comfort at the same time. Affection carried static. Any touch could turn.

People called me "guarded," "hard," "a little intense."

They didn't see the girl standing inside my skin, backed into a corner, holding a lifetime of memories like a stack of plates she couldn't afford to drop.

On paper, I was stable now.

I had a job.

I had four walls.

I had a lock.

Inside, everything still shook.

I'd tell myself: *You're safe now.*

My body would answer back: *Prove it.*

CHAPTER TWENTY-NINE

The Fire I Walked Back Into

***

The first time I really wrote about my life, it felt like walking back into a burning house on purpose.

Nobody ordered me to do it.

No judge.

No caseworker.

No therapist with a clipboard.

One night, the apartment was too quiet, the ghosts were too loud, and I was tired of being nothing but a reaction to what had happened.

So I sat down with a cheap notebook and a pen that skipped when I pressed too hard.

For a minute, I just stared at the blank page.

My hand hovered, shaking a little.

It would've been easier to keep scrolling on my phone, to turn on the TV, to dig around in the fridge for something to eat I didn't even want. Anything but open the door in my head I'd spent years nailing shut.

But some stubborn piece of me—the same part that had kept walking through every foster house and courthouse and empty driveway—leaned forward.

Fine, I thought. *Let's see what happens.*

I started with one memory.

Not the worst one.

Not the "headline" trauma.

Just a moment that had stuck: tiny me in the flowerbed, my mother on the horse, the ground rushing up.

I wrote it the way I remembered it, not the way anyone else would have told it. The feel of the dirt under my nails. The sound of hooves before I saw them. The way my sister's scream sounded different from any other noise that day.

My hand cramped.

The letters came out uneven.

But once I started, it was like something inside me refused to stop.

I wrote the camper.

The fire.

The knife at the door.

The bullet through the window.

The Victorian house.

My mother naked and screaming.

Being left alone for days.

The pig farm that almost felt like love.

Arizona.

The group home.

The field.

The apartment.

Not in the "appropriate" order adults had always used when they tried to summarize me.

In *my* order.

The way it actually lived in my bones.

Sometimes I had to stop because my hand shook too hard, or the words blurred, or my chest felt too tight. I'd get up, walk the apartment, check the locks, run cold water over my wrists until the echo of someone's yelling faded.

Then I'd sit back down and keep going.

It didn't feel noble.
It didn't feel triumphant.

It felt like dragging myself, piece by piece, out of a burning house where everybody else had already decided I was the problem.

And still, with every scene I put on paper, something shifted.

The story wasn't just trapped in me anymore.

It was outside of me, in ink and paper, where I could look at it and say:

That happened.
And I survived it.

Not "maybe it wasn't that bad."
Not "maybe I imagined it."
Not "maybe I'm just dramatic."

No.

That happened.

Writing didn't magically fix my nervous system.
It didn't stop the nightmares.
It didn't make the past less brutal.

But it did something just as important:

It put me back in the center of my own story.

I stopped being just "the girl that no one claimed."

I started to become the woman who could claim *herself.*

CHAPTER THIRTY

Claiming

***

*P*eople ask, "Why tell it? Why write it down at all?"

Because for most of my life, everyone else told my story for me.

My mother told it as, "She burned the house down."

My sister told it as, "You deserve to die."

The foster system told it as, "Behavioral issues, dramatic, runaway."

Parts of my family told it as, "She lied and put her father in prison."

Even the "good" adults—teachers, caseworkers, counselors—flattened it into bullet points:

- History of trauma
- Multiple placements
- Sexual abuse confirmed
- Father incarcerated

Those lists might've helped them move me from file to file, from house to house.

They didn't help me understand who I was.

So I wrote for the girl who sat at the top of the fold-out ladder, listening to threats downstairs.

For the girl brushing glass out of her hair.

For the girl locked in a house alone.

For the girl in the group home bed, staring at a

ceiling that didn't belong to her.
For the girl sleeping in a car, pretending it was temporary.

For every version of me who looked around and thought:

If this is family, what does it mean that nobody wants me?

I wrote this for them.
And I wrote it for you.

For the kid who got called "dramatic" when you were really just drowning.
For the teenager everyone labeled "trouble" because it was easier than asking, *What happened to you?*
For the adult who still flinches at sounds you "should be over" by now.

If nobody has ever said it to you and meant it, let me say it here:

You deserved better.
You still do.

You deserved adults who chose you over their addictions, their pride, their reputations.
You deserved a home that didn't require hypervigilance to survive.
You deserved a childhood, not a war zone.

None of this is your fault.
Not the chaos you were born into.
Not the fucked-up choices of the adults who were supposed to protect you.

Not the lies they told about you to keep from facing what they did.

You are not too broken.
You are not "too much."
You are not imaginary.

You are proof that a person can grow in the cracks between disasters and still stand.

This isn't a neat story.

There's no perfect redemption arc where everything gets fixed and tied up with a ribbon. My life didn't suddenly turn into a Hallmark movie when I got four walls and a key.

I still have bad days.
I still have triggers.
I still have moments where the girl inside me—six, eight, eleven, fourteen—panics and wants to bolt.

But now, when those ghosts show up, I have something that child never did:

My own voice.

I can say, out loud if I have to:

That happened.
It was wrong.
It was not my fault.
And I am still here.

This book is not a list of complaints.
It's not revenge.

It's a record.

Of what it costs a child to live through the things people don't want to look at.
Of how survival becomes adulthood, whether you're ready or not.
Of how, piece by bloody piece, you can pull

yourself out from under the weight of other people's
choices and decide who you are.

I was the girl that no one claimed.

Now, sentence by sentence, life by life,
I am claiming myself.

And this—putting it in order, in ink, in my
words—

this is only the beginning.

EPILOGUE

The Girl I Claimed

The first time I realized I'd really broken the cycle,

it wasn't in a therapist's office or over some big life milestone.

It was in my kitchen.

The window over the sink was open, curtains breathing in and out with the evening air. A pot was boiling over on the stove because I'd gotten distracted, the hiss of water hitting the burner filling the room.

Behind me, a glass slipped out of a small hand and shattered on the floor.

My child froze.

Big eyes.

Held breath.

Body pinned in place like they were waiting for impact.

I felt it all at once:

Every kitchen I'd ever stood in.

The heat of the grease fire.

The crack of a glass hitting the wall.

My mother's voice, sharp as broken dishes.

My father's rage.

For a split second, those ghosts stepped into my kitchen like they owned it.

I had a choice.
I could let their voices speak through me
or I could do something no one ever did for me.
I turned off the burner.
Then I put the dish towel down.
Stepped carefully over the glass.
Knelt so I was eye-level with the small, shaking
person in front of me.

"Hey," I said softly. "You okay?"

They nodded, eyes shining.

"I'm sorry," they whispered. "I didn't mean to—
"

"I know," I said. "It was an accident. You're not
in trouble. Stay right there so you don't cut your
feet, okay? I'll clean it up."

Their shoulders sagged with relief so fast it
almost broke my heart.

I cleaned up the glass.

We swept.
We laughed a little.
We wiped the floor until it was safe again.

Later that night, after everyone was in bed and
the house had gone quiet, I sat alone at the table and
let it hit me.

That was it.

That was the thing I never got as a kid:

An adult who stayed calm when something
broke.
Someone who asked if I was okay instead of telling
me I'd ruined everything.
A voice that said, "You're safe. We can fix this."

Nobody did that for me.

But I had done it for my child.

Right there in that kitchen, barefoot on a floor that used to hold my fear, I felt something unhook inside me.

I will not be perfect.

I will mess up.

I will get tired and say the wrong thing and have to apologize.

But I will not be them.

The girl that no one claimed had grown up and claimed herself—
and with that, she'd claimed the right to raise love in a different shape.

Not in fear.

Not in a war.

Not in silence.

In truth.

In choice.

In the simple, stubborn act of staying.

There are still days when I hear a tone in someone's voice and my whole body braces. Still nights when an old nightmare drags me back through a door I thought I'd nailed shut. Still moments when a random smell motor oil, cigarette smoke, damp wood puts me right back in a house I haven't set foot in for decades.

Healing isn't a straight line.

It's a spiral.

You circle the same places, but a little farther out each time.
The memories don't vanish.
They just stop driving the car.

I used to think my story was nothing but damage.

Now I know it's also proof.

Proof that you can be born into wreckage and still choose calm.
That you can be raised in violence and still choose gentleness.
That you can be lied about, doubted, moved, renamed, and left—

and still stand up and say:
This happened.
It didn't destroy me.
I get to decide who I am now.

I was the girl that no one claimed.

But I am the woman who claimed that girl
who took her by the hand, led her out of the burning houses and the empty driveways and the haunted bedrooms,
and told her:

"We can go now.
They don't get the last word.
We do."

And this book
—these pages, these scenes, these names and nights and houses is me keeping that promise.
To her.
To me.

To anyone who's ever been told their story was "too much" to believe.

You are not too much.

Your story is not too big.

And you?

You are worth claiming.

About the Author

***

Paige grew up in more houses than she can easily count - campers and cabins, Victorian ghosts and foster care couches, group homes and cheap apartment with wheels and thick silence.

She aged out of a system that rarely believed her, carrying scars that didn't show up on paperwork. For years, she worked, raised a family, and held her story inside like a secret that burned every time she swallowed it back down.

This book is the result of finally stopping the swallow.

Today, Paige is a woman who pays her own bills, keeps a key on her own ring, and knows exactly where every door in her life leads because she chose them. She works, parents, loves, and laughs louder than anyone who's spent time in the dark is "supposed" to.

She wrote *The Girl That No One Claimed* series for the kid she used to be, and for every person who's ever been told they were too dramatic, too broken, or too unbelievable.

She is living proof that your past can explain you without ever being allowed to define you.

Watch for *The Girl That No One Claimed: When Hell Comes Back* for the continuation of her life and the fallout of raising herself without the support of counseling and guidance.

9 798995 122708